# SPIRITUAL WARFARE

## FOR EVERY CHRISTIAN

# SPIRITUAL WARFARE

## FOR EVERY CHRISTIAN

*How To Live in Victory
and Retake the Land*

# DEAN SHERMAN

*with Bill Payne*

FOREWORD BY JOHN DAWSON

**Frontline Communications**
A Division of Youth With A Mission
P.O. Box 55787, Seattle, WA 98155
(206) 771-1153

2019181716151413121110987654321
99989796959493929190

ISBN 0-92754-505-5

To my dad, Byron Sherman, who demonstrated balance and endurance, and my
mom, Viola Sherman, who taught me to
love God and resist evil.

# Acknowledgments

I am grateful to God for allowing me by His grace to minister and learn these principles through trial and error. I'm indebted to Loren Cunningham and my other colleagues in Youth With A Mission for their encouragement and trust over the past 23 years. Thank you to all those in the Body of Christ who have graciously acknowledged being helped by this teaching and thanks to those who encouraged me to write it down for others to read.

Bill Payne gave himself tirelessly to seeing the speaking style transformed to print. Special thanks to Pastor Mario Sassi and New Covenant Assembly of London, Ontario, Canada, who supported Bill during this time. Others to whom I am grateful: Warren Keapproth, who typed many hours of tapes to transcript; Janice Rogers spent hundreds of hours editing; Jim Rogers and Jim Shaw of Frontline Communications, Editorial Division in Texas helped edit, proofread, and typeset the material. Thanks also to Juanita Barton, Bill Eaton, Pandora Patton, Meredith Puff, Patricia Rupprecht, and Pam Warren.

My deepest love and thanks go to my wife Michelle, and my children Troy and Cherie, for walking the path of warfare with me.

Dean Sherman
Kailua-Kona, Hawaii
September, 1990

# Foreword

When I finished reading this manuscript, I got down on my knees and thanked God. My soul was filled again with reverence for my loving Heavenly Father. His character is matchless and His plan is perfect. Dean Sherman has given us a thorough and balanced teaching that is full of insight, yet laced with humor and easy to read. The truth explored in this book should lay foundations on which a believer's life is built. I can't wait to read this book to my family and to recommend it to my friends.

I have counted Dean as one of my closest friends and though I have not heard him teach on most of this material, it is familiar to me because I have seen him live it with integrity. The revelation in this book has not come cheaply. The sorrows and victories of twenty-three years of missionary work have been poured into it like precious fragrance into a perfume bottle. We have needed this book. It is one of the few truly important books for every category of believer to own and to read periodically.

John Dawson
Lakeview Terrace, California
September, 1990

# CONTENTS

# CHAPTER ONE

## A Life and Death Struggle

I was lying on the bare floorboards of our house in Port Moresby, Papua New Guinea. The year was 1970. For seven days I had been fasting and praying; I had to have some answers.

We had been there for three months, and though our Youth With A Mission team was witnessing and holding meetings in the marketplaces, we were seeing few results. And I had noticed something else—something that really bothered me. Although churches in this city were full and thousands claimed to be born again, they were still bound by sin. Many so-called Christians continued to practice witchcraft. And even when we preached against it, there was no change. There was only hardness. Something was very wrong. So I began to fast and pray, asking God for some answers.

One day as I lay praying on that rough floor, God's voice spoke into my mind. His answer was unexpected—something entirely new to my thinking. Yet it was as clear as I have ever heard Him speak:

*Praise is the key to breaking down the forces of darkness which have held this city since the beginning of time. These forces have never been challenged.*

I lay there stunned. I had never thought about spiritual forces controlling a place—no one I knew in 1970 was speaking about powers of darkness over cities. I had never heard teaching on spiritual warfare, and was only aware of a few people who "specialized" in ministries of delivering people from demons.

Then I realized something else as I lay there, pondering what God had said.

The Church in New Guinea was well-established. It had thrived to a degree. Missionaries had spent years building the Church of Jesus Christ. They had right doctrine and believed the Bible. Yet God said the spiritual forces over Papua New Guinea *had never been challenged*. That meant the Church could have measurable success without ever directly challenging the powers of darkness! My mind reeled with the possibilities.

I asked God to confirm that it had been His voice, and not my imagination. After sharing with the other YWAM leaders on our team, Tom Hallas and Kalafi Moala, they too believed it was from the Lord. Still it was so new that I asked God for further reassurance.

A few days later, a car pulled up in front of our house and out stepped a sweaty, lanky, American.

"Bless God, brothers! I've been lookin' for some Christians...." he whooped, pumping our arms. "I described the kind I was lookin' for all over town and everyone pointed up to this house! Praise God!"

I swallowed, casting a sidelong glance at Tom and Kalafi. So the people in town thought this boisterous evangelist was our kind, eh? But we welcomed him to begin a series of meetings in our house.

He preached to the few who came up the hill and brandished a tambourine in the times of singing. When he prayed, he shouted at the top of his voice, imploring God to save people, to heal, and to fill people with the Holy Ghost. Not the Holy Spirit...the Holy *Ghost*.

Despite his peculiarities, however, something told us he was okay. What happened at the meeting on the second night was the real clincher. The preacher stood before our little group, eyes tightly closed, and proclaimed in his prophecy voice, "Yea, the Lord would say that praise is the key to breaking through the forces of darkness over this city!"

Wow, I thought. The same thing God had said to me when I was fasting and praying!

A few weeks later, a Dutch evangelist came through. He also gave a direct word from God to us: "Praise is the key to breaking down the forces of darkness!" A third came, from New Zealand, and a fourth from Australia—all said the same thing. Four men from four nations came within weeks, each using the same terminology that the Lord had spoken to me on the floor that day.

It didn't take a rocket scientist to understand God had spoken. We put it into practice, becoming fanatical "praisers." Sometimes we worshiped God in our little mission house all morning. We marched around the room, sang at the top of our voices, shouted praises, and fell to our knees or stretched out face down, praising God. And it started making a difference, for we were finally seeing breakthroughs, with people getting saved, set free from bondage, and coming into the fullness of the Spirit.

When we went out to evangelize, the change was clear. Instead of hardened, unrepentant people hiding behind a Christianized facade, we saw individuals stand weeping publicly, renouncing their witchcraft. The trickle of converts increased to a steady flow, and we had as many as five thousand attending our meetings. Every week we baptized new Christians in the ocean—and this continued for three years. Cripples got up and walked and blind people were healed. Within six months, we saw nine fellowships of Spirit-filled believers begun in Port Moresby. We were riding on the crest of a wave.

However, we were soon to find out how real...deadly real...spiritual warfare is. Satan's attack was sudden and vicious.

David Wallis, a New Zealander in his early 20s, was on our team. During the height of this spiritual move, he led several other young men out to evangelize an outlying village. They encountered fierce opposition from the local witch doctor. When they refused to leave, the shaman put a curse on them.

After six weeks, the team returned to Port Moresby. David didn't think anything about the curse, nor did we. Many times witch doctors had cursed us and our efforts, but without any effect. However, David reported that he had suffered from a fever off and on while away in the village. The fever was gone now, but he was weak. When I suggested he see a doctor, he said he felt better and just needed to rest.

Yet after a couple of days of bed rest, David grew weaker. And his fever returned. Then one day, about three days after he returned from the village, I went into the room where David lay on his bed. He was delirious, had a high fever, and was babbling incoherently. We immediately rushed him to the hospital. But we were not prepared for the devastating news: We were told David was in an advanced stage of cerebral malaria. I asked, "How can that be? There isn't supposed to be any malaria in this part of Papua New Guinea." But they were certain—and the prognosis couldn't have been more grim, either. The doctor informed us that this was the most deadly form of malaria. There was only a slight chance that David would live, and even if he did, the damage to his brain would leave him in a permanently vegetative state.

Our team went home and began a desperate vigil of prayer and fasting. It was a heavy struggle as we prayed through the night—there was such a feeling of oppression. Before this we had been able to pray for hours, yet here we were in the greatest need and we could hardly form the words. To me, it seemed like my prayers came out of my mouth and just fell on my chest. It was as if all the powers of hell had centered their might against us, focusing their fury on the body of David Wallis.

By morning, however, I believed we had made some head-way spiritually. I rushed to the hospital only to find David's bed freshly made up. He was gone. When I looked for the matron, she crisply informed me that David was in intensive care. He was convulsing. She said, "He's going to die and it's your fault—you and your religious convictions have cost this man his life! And even if he does live, he'll be a vegetable!"

I tried to explain that we had tried to get him to come earlier, that we weren't one of those groups who didn't believe in going to doctors, but she wouldn't listen. The entire hospital staff seemed convinced that we were religious kooks, and should be held legally responsible for this young man's condition.

I went home reeling. What if David died? Would they prosecute us? And even if they didn't, would our reputation be so ruined in this relatively small city that our ministry couldn't continue? And what would happen to all our young converts— what would this do to their faith? Hadn't we told them that God works miracles today, that we had authority over the forces of darkness through Jesus Christ?

The hospital called David's family in New Zealand and his father flew to his bedside. He didn't say much at our first meeting, but he did remind me that he had warned David not to go with us. "I told him you were an irresponsible bunch!" he said.

At the end of the second day, the medical staff again told me there was no hope for David. I went into his sickroom and there he lay unconscious, curled into a fetal position and as yellow as a cube of butter. Various tubes were connected to him and the swish and hum of a breathing machine kept his chest moving slightly. Otherwise he was as still as death.

Summoning all the faith I could muster, I desperately but softly cried out to God. Then, following an impulse, I knelt down beside his bed and spoke directly into David's ear:

"You demon power of death! I rebuke you in the name of Jesus and command you to loose your hold on this man's body!"

The moment I said that, there was a strong gurgling from his mouth. And that was all. I returned home and again we spent the entire night in prayer.

When I returned the next morning, I hurried to intensive care. As I walked in, David was sitting up! He did not have the breathing tube in his mouth, but the intravenous tubes remained. His father turned and faced me with a despairing look. Then I looked into David's eyes: There was only a blank stare.

"I've been here, calling him by name all morning," his father wearily explained. "Nothing...no response at all."

I looked for the matron and asked about David's condition. "He's worse!" she declared.

"But yesterday he was lying in a fetal position," I protested, "and today he's sitting up, without the oxygen tubes! He's better, he has to be."

She remained adamant. He was no better. He would never be normal again. It was a tragedy, what had happened to this young man, and it was all our fault.

I returned to his room and David's father walked out, leaving me alone with him. As I walked around the end of his bed, I noticed his blank eyes were following me. I said, "David, we are praying for you and Jesus has the victory!" Then an unbelievable thing happened. If I hadn't seen and heard it myself, I would have trouble believing it. Without his lips moving or that blank stare leaving his eyes, the word "Hallelujah" came from his throat. I left to go back and report to the team. Surely God had heard us.

When I returned the next day, David had been moved from intensive care. Though extremely weak, he was talking intelligently and walking with a little help. I could hardly keep from jumping up and down and shouting "Praise the Lord" for the entire hospital to hear! Let them think we were fanatics—God had given us the victory!

That was twenty years ago. And since that time David Wallis has been a missionary in South India. Yet for me, this experience was much more than a marvelous healing of a very sick young man. Through our desperate prayer and fasting, God had allowed us to have a part in changing Port Moresby—a city of seventy-five thousand souls. Not that we were the only ones; I'm sure God had other intercessors as well. But our prayers helped push back the forces of darkness impeding the evangelization of that place. In a city that, at the time, had only five people who claimed to be Spirit-filled, now there are five large Charismatic congregations, as well as vital renewal movements in the Roman Catholic, Anglican, and United churches.

We almost had a casualty. But Jesus had given us the victory, and He had stirred my interest in the whole matter of spiritual warfare. It was the beginning of a quest. I began to pray and search the Scriptures. Since I was in a traveling ministry, I talked to missionaries and leaders. And I began to see contrasts everywhere I went. There were hard, cold places, sometimes bordering areas which were spiritually thriving. For instance, you can stand on the border between Kenya and Somalia, with your toes in one country and your heels in the other. In Kenya, there are 16 million Christians—a majority of the population. However, in Somalia, Christians number less than 1% of the population, and most of these are foreign residents. I couldn't help but wonder why.

I saw similar contrasts between cities, between neighborhoods, even between Christian families, and individuals, and their ability to live overcoming lives. Could it be that we were missing something...something very big and powerful?

An answer began to emerge. I became very excited as I began to see what every Christian had at his or her disposal—the power to walk in personal victory, and the power to reach the world, setting communities and nations free from bondage. This was more than a fringe subject—I began to see that we are all called to be warriors, and we must all learn how to fight.

# CHAPTER TWO

## The Greatest Adventure

Who doesn't enjoy watching a good movie, a fast-paced TV program, or curling up with a gripping book? Or how about the excitement of being in the stands at a closely matched sporting event? Almost everyone loves the unfolding of a story or the staging of a competitive challenge. We invest a great deal of time and money watching actors pretend to be something they're not. We burn with indignation when the villain crushes the innocent. We hold our breath for the good guys and cheer when the hero vanquishes evil. We also shout in victory when our team tramples the other team to score a goal.

Whether through fiction or sports, there is something deep within that derives vicarious pleasure from seeing two forces meet in battle. Why do we have such a tremendous desire for these forms of entertainment? We long for conflict, adventure, and excitement because we were created to be actively involved in the ultimate conflict—the battle between good and evil. Our nature demands that we take sides in any fight, and root for one side or the other. God intended us to be involved in conflict, fighting for righteousness. We were meant to be actively destroying those things that would hinder or corrupt the Kingdom of God, pushing back the powers of darkness.

We can enter into the greatest battle of all, the greatest adventure. We can see good triumph over evil and prisoners set free. This is not the plot of a book or the theme of a movie. It is exactly what God intended for us. It can become reality when we learn how to engage in spiritual warfare.

Unfortunately, most people stumble into this battle unknowingly. Every person born into this world is immersed in spiritual warfare. Having been plunged into the conflict of the ages, we cannot be exempt or neutral. We will either be trampled by malign forces or we will be victorious, winning souls, changing society, influencing history, and helping establish the Kingdom of God through spiritual warfare.

People often say to me: "Since you teach on spiritual warfare, the devil must really be after you!" But if I get to thinking that I am a special case, I open myself both to attack from the enemy and to spiritual pride. I do not believe that Satan is more concerned with me than with any other Christian. We all have the same potential for victory or defeat. The devil is equally threatened and equally defeated by each and every Christian who stands in Christ's victory and consistently practices the principles of spiritual warfare.

I have been asked many times why I teach on spiritual warfare. I don't speak from a position of special revelation and authority. It is not because I was set apart by God to deliver a message. Nor do I teach this subject because I am an expert or have made a lifelong study of these principles. I have no special gifting nor calling in relation to the principles of spiritual warfare—I teach on a large number of other topics with equal enthusiasm. And I am not a demon chaser, blaming demonic forces for every uncomfortable situation or flaw in someone's character.

I teach about spiritual warfare first of all because it is a major ingredient missing in today's efforts of world evangelization. We simply have not dealt with the powers of darkness to the degree that we should as Christ's church, living in the victory of Jesus' name and in the power of the Holy Spirit.

The second reason I teach on spiritual warfare comes from my involvement in counseling. I have noticed that Christians in general tend to allow a defeated enemy to steal the victory that Christ won for them on the Cross.

Finally, I speak on spiritual warfare because God has emphasized it throughout history. He is still emphasizing it. He wants His people to be an army that influences the world and drives back the powers of darkness.

## Ready or Not...You're in the Battle

I find many are simply not interested in hearing about spiritual warfare. They would never come to a seminar, listen to a tape, nor read this or any other book that deals with the enemy. Some feel that spiritual warfare is a special gift or calling only for a small segment of Christians. I remember one lady in Australia saying, "Well, I'm just not the fighting type."

Spiritual warfare, however, has nothing to do with personality, gifting, calling, or background. When we signed up to be Christians, we automatically entered into warfare. It's not a matter of preference. Spiritual warfare begins with recognizing that we are already in the midst of it.

Almost every Christian freely confesses that Jesus defeated the enemy at Calvary; however, the mental knowledge that Jesus defeated the devil and that we have authority over him isn't enough. We continually allow Satan, whom we know was defeated, to push us around and take advantage of us. We often act more like victims than the victors Christ intended us to be.

As the children of God, we need never be victims. If we understand the biblical principles of spiritual warfare and how the enemy operates, and if we stand against him, we will overcome.

## "The Devil Made Me Do It!"

Like many other areas in Christianity, spiritual warfare is in great need of balance. When it comes to spiritual warfare, people tend toward two extremes: overemphasis or underemphasis.

Perhaps you have seen people who overemphasize spiritual warfare. They see demons in everything. If your wife is cranky, it's a demon. If the car won't start, it's a demon. Every bump and scrape and minor incident is the work of a demon. It seems like everyone they know has demons. They can discern how many there are and they usually know their names. Every problem is solved by casting out a demon, and they cast them out at every opportunity. They cast out demons of clumsiness, demons of tooth decay, even demons of high mortgage payments! These well-meaning people totally eliminate any sense of personal responsibility by calling every wrong choice and every selfish, sinful action the handiwork of the devil and his cohorts.

Those who overemphasize demons are often ignoring the victory that is available. They live in constant conflict with the demons, and because of their preoccupation, with many people as well. Every Christian is meant to live in continuous victory through Jesus Christ. We must be convinced of this and not see demons in every situation and behavior.

In any ministry situation, we tend to cling to our successes. When we have ministered successfully in healing or deliverance, or when we have received a new and exciting teaching, we tend to camp around that success, that teaching, that formula, that ministry. We can so embrace a single idea or method that we exclude everything else. We can even allow ourselves to withdraw from other Christians and other points of view. We become isolated and exclusive, saying, "I have the answer— only I have the key." That is spiritual pride.

No one is immune to spiritual pride. We are all prone to that inner desire for power, control, and recognition. Some years ago while still in New Guinea, this happened to me. One day when I placed my hand on a man's head to pray for him, he fell down on the floor, thrashing about and foaming at the mouth. It was very dramatic. I proceeded to command the demon in him to leave, which it did. I looked at my hand in amazement: What power! I thought I must have broken through into a new level of spirituality. I could make things happen!

I didn't realize it at the time, but I had become more enamored with the process than with the results. And Satan accommodated me. Everywhere I went over the next several months there were demonic manifestations in people. But finally, I began to notice that the people for whom I prayed were not remaining free—sometimes the results were not life-changing and permanent.

I had been taken in. I suddenly realized that I would have been disappointed if someone had quietly and instantly been set free without my doing anything. And that was wrong.

We must be careful. If we are unbalanced in our desire to see a supernatural manifestation, Satan will be happy to put on a show for us. God, however, is not interested in performing to satisfy our selfish interests.

I am a strong believer in setting people free from demonic bondage. However, spiritual warfare should never be an end in itself, but merely a means to an end. We must keep our focus on God's priorities, as Jesus did when He was on earth. God is always doing two things: He is reconciling the lost to Himself through His son Jesus Christ (world evangelism), and He is bringing His body, the Church, to unity, maturity, and wholeness.

As we work toward these two goals, we will come across those who are in bondage and need deliverance. Of course, we must reach out in love and set them free. But then we should move on, keeping our focus on the goals of God. Jesus told us in Mark 16:15 to go and give His gospel to every person, adding almost as a postscript in verses 17 and 18 that we would also heal people and cast out demons. Needy people were Jesus' focus, not the supernatural fireworks.

### "If We Don't Talk About Him, Maybe He'll Go Away!"

An underemphasis of spiritual warfare principles is just as unbalanced as an overemphasis. In every town where the "overemphasis groups" reside, there is at least one group of the other extreme. They are turned off and even frightened by those who cast out demons all over town. Their understandable distaste drives them to a position of denial.

A friend of mine took a team to minister in a large, non-Christian nation in Asia where there was much demonic activity and witchcraft. To my friend's surprise, the pastor of their host church asked them not to mention the words "devil" or "demons" in his church or while praying with people. "When you talk about the devil, all sorts of things start going wrong," the pastor of this Pentecostal church explained. "Besides, we don't want to be like those people who see demons in everything!"

This is not unusual. Many are convinced that if they think or talk about the enemy, they will become vulnerable to his attacks, as if any acknowledgment of Satan were an invitation for demonic activity. If they mention him at all, it's usually a quick and loud declaration of victory. They couch their opinions in quaint remarks, like:

"Praise God! We have the victory. Amen?"

...or:

"Jesus defeated the devil 2,000 years ago."

...and:

"He's a lion, but his teeth have been pulled."

...or that old favorite:

"I've read the back of the book (the Bible) and we win."

They sound like they are trying to convince themselves as much as anyone else.

Our victory has never been in question, and it is not fragile. What Christ did on the Cross was for all time and for all people, if they will accept and embrace it. We need not fear knowledge, even if the knowledge is about our enemy. No army has suffered from too much understanding in the ways of its enemies. We can relax in confident victory and still know the truth about the devil, his tactics, and his strategies.

We definitely should not ignore him, or pretend he does not exist, hoping he will go away. It's like a small child covering his eyes and shouting, "You can't see me! You can't find me!" The devil doesn't go away just because we don't believe in him. He will not leave us alone just because we leave him alone. In spiritual warfare, ignorance is not bliss. Ignorance can lead to bondage. The devil works in darkness. When we are ignorant of him, we too are in darkness, and he is free to work. But the more we shine the light on his activities, the more his work is hindered.

We can be sure that Satan knows who his enemies are, and that he continually arms himself with information about us. He

knows about us if we are being effective for Jesus. The demo-
niac said in Acts 19:15, just before he pounced upon those who
sought to exercise power over him, "I recognize Jesus, and I
know about Paul, but who are you?" Satan knows those who
continually, consistently exercise their God-given authority and
the biblical principles of spiritual warfare. He also knows those
who hide behind empty words, with little or no conviction of
victory. We need to take our hands from our eyes and confront
the truth.

John chapter eight says, "You shall know the truth, and the
truth shall make you free." Do we really believe that truth sets
us free? If so, what truth? All truth? How about the truth
concerning the powers of darkness? Does that truth set us free?

Everything we know about the enemy comes from the same
source from which we learn about God: the Bible—the Word
of God, inspired by the Holy Spirit. The Bible proclaims that
all Scripture is edifying, and doesn't worry about giving the
devil too much publicity. If the Word of God takes time to
acknowledge the devil and reveal his schemes, we must give
those portions of biblical truth equal time and consideration.
Even the truth about the enemy can make us free. It is not
dangerous to know all that the Bible teaches us about the enemy;
it is dangerous to remain ignorant of what the Bible says.

On the other hand, the only reliable source of information
concerning powers of darkness is the Bible. Our beliefs and
doctrines concerning the devil should never be based on our
experiences or on the testimony of demons. There are those who
claim an intimate and exclusive knowledge of the enemy,
derived from their experience during deliverance sessions and
their conversations with those bound by demons. When it comes
to spiritual warfare, if it's not in the Bible, be careful.

### Aware of The Devil, Impressed With God

Many live in fear of the enemy. They are truly frightened
of what the devil will do to them, their families, and their
churches. In one place where I often speak, a pastor said to me,
"Dean, I'm concerned about your teaching so many people on
spiritual warfare. People don't realize what they're getting

into!" He went on to tell how his church had gotten involved ministering to former warlocks and witches. Suddenly one of their church elders had a broken marriage, another had a heart attack, and another almost had a nervous breakdown. "You're encouraging people to go into a very dangerous area," he warned.

Because I have such respect for this pastor, I took his words to heart, and began to pray and again, search the Scriptures. But where was this fear in the Bible? I could find nothing in God's Word that said we were to be afraid of spiritual warfare, or that we would be at the mercy of evil forces if we challenged the devil. Instead the Bible says over 300 times "Fear not!" and Psalm 23:4 says, "I will fear no evil: for thou art with me" (KJV). (See also Heb. 2:14-15.)

Satan loves to bring fear to people. Fear grows in the absence of knowing who God is. To be effective in spiritual warfare, to be balanced and free from fear, we must be *aware* of the enemy but *impressed* with God. It should never be the other way around. We should not be impressed with Satan and only aware of God. If we aren't careful, our conversations can focus on the amazing powers of darkness, and what all the devil is doing. One young lady told me with tremendous enthusiasm that 30 witches' covens were recently discovered within her little town. I answered, "It's a good thing there aren't 31."

While we should never be awestruck by the enemy's activities, we must learn to see what he's trying to do in our lives. We must be able to say, "This is a move of the enemy," or "The devil is behind this." If we can recognize the devil's attempts to hinder us and those around us, we will know where, when, and how to act.

How can we know when it is the devil, and not just circumstances? How can we avoid that extreme of seeing demons behind everything that goes wrong? The answer is to simply *ask God*. Don't assume that it is the devil's work, but don't refuse to acknowledge that it may be his doing. Just ask God to show you what is going on. He has promised to guide us. The gift of discerning of spirits, promised in I Corinthians 12:10, is God showing us what is going on in the spirit realm at any given time. (Heb. 5:14)

Being impressed with God is the other side of the coin. We must be far more enthusiastic about learning all that we can about God. If we know much about the devil but little about God, we will be ineffective, not just in spiritual warfare, but in every area of our lives. If we are going to study the enemy, we must first know the truth about God. We will never fear the devil if we know that God is sovereign, immeasurably great and powerful, yet kind, gentle, and unswerving in His love and commitment to us.

Another truth with which we must equip ourselves is: who we are in Christ. Satan preys upon those who do not know their position in Christ or their relationship with God. To say we are Christians is not enough. We must believe God in His declaration of who we are. We must know and believe what the Bible says about us in order to live out that reality and walk with that authority.

When we know who we are, the enemy is forced to retreat from us as confident children of the living God. Thousands of Christians are daily pushed about by the devil, becoming victims of circumstances, of people, or of wrong concepts. They should be walking in the knowledge of who they are in Christ, humbly acknowledging with confidence: "I know who I am; therefore, Satan, you cannot do these things to me."

This understanding came to me as I searched God's Word concerning spiritual warfare. The book of Ephesians came alive to me. Consider the following verses:

*Finally, be strong in the Lord, and in the strength of His might. Put on the full armor of God, that you may be able to stand firm against the schemes of the devil. For our struggle is not against flesh and blood, but against the rulers, against the powers, against the world-forces of this darkness, against the spiritual forces of wickedness in the heavenly places. Therefore take up the full armor of God, that you may be able to resist in the evil day, and having done everything, to stand firm. Stand firm therefore, having girded your loins with truth, and having put on the breastplate of truth, and righteousness, and having shod your feet with the preparation of the gospel of peace; in addition to all, taking up the shield of faith with which you will be able to extinguish all the flaming missiles of the evil one. And take the helmet of salvation, and the sword of the Spirit, which is the Word of God. With all prayer and petition pray at all times in the Spirit, and with this in view, be on the alert with all perseverance and petition for all the saints, and pray on my behalf, that utterance may be given to me in the opening of my mouth, to make known with boldness the mystery of the gospel, for which I am an ambassador in chains; that in proclaiming it I may speak boldly, as I ought to speak (Eph. 6:10-20).*

Verse 10 of Ephesians 6 reads, "Finally, be strong in the Lord." The word "finally" indicates that being strong in the Lord is the last element in a series of important principles of spiritual warfare. What precedes the "finally" is the vitally important focus of Ephesians. Paul is reminding us that we can't be strong in the Lord until we have embraced all that comes before. So in order to understand the word "finally," and what it means to "be strong," we need to know what principles have been laid out in the book of Ephesians.

Watchman Nee wrote a commentary on the book of Ephesians called *Sit, Walk, Stand*. I would like to borrow his apt title to illustrate the three major messages of Ephesians. Paul lays elementary foundations for the Christian life in three segments: sitting, walking, and standing.

## Sitting

Ephesians 1-3 focuses on our position in Christ and our relationship with God. It is an account of what God has done to forgive and reconcile us. These chapters are full of declarations of *who we are* based on *what God has done*. God has "blessed us with every spiritual blessing." He "chose us in Him before the foundation of the world." He "predestined us to adoption as sons through Jesus Christ to Himself." He "lavished" grace upon us. In Him we have "redemption through His blood, the forgiveness of our trespasses." "He made known to us the mystery of His will." "We have obtained an inheritance." We were "sealed in Him." We were dead but God made us "alive together with Christ." He washed us and has forgiven us. We have been saved "by grace...and that not of ourselves...not as a result of works, that no one should boast." Once separated and far off, we "have been brought near by the blood of Christ." Christ is "our peace," and through Him we have "access in one Spirit to the Father." We are "no longer strangers" but "fellow-citizens...and are of God's household."

This is who we are: recipients of all these wonderful benefits from God. And it culminates in God making us sit "with Him in the heavenly places." It is almost too much to believe, but God's Word declares it. Reading the book of Ephesians should establish us in unshakable confidence. However, it's not enough to read these Scriptures. Christianity is not one-dimensional. It has never been enough to simply believe in a set of doctrines written on a piece of paper. What we believe, we must also live out. We must embrace these truths, believe them, and learn to sit with God.

Being seated speaks of three things. It speaks of *reigning*. "Those who receive the abundance of grace and of the gift of righteousness will reign in life through the one Jesus Christ" (Rom. 5:17). We are meant to reign in life. We must ask ourselves: Are we reigning, or are we slaves to our circumstances and the attacks of the enemy?

Being seated also speaks of *a finished work*. We only sit after the work is complete. God is saying through Ephesians that everything has already been done to make us what we need to be. It is a finished work. Having completed the work of atonement, having defeated the devil, having spoiled all principalities and powers, having established Himself as the reigning King of Kings, Jesus took His rightful place and sat down. We too need to take our rightful place, the place won for us by our glorious Lord and Savior, and sit down. Our salvation is complete; our authority over the enemy has been won. (Col. 2:10)

Finally, being seated speaks of being in *a relaxed position*. Relaxing is the natural response when a job is completed. When we are convinced that nothing can undo the completed work, we can relax. We need more Christians who know they are kept by the power of God, Christians who know they are saved and secure in Christ, being seated with Him in the heavenly places.

# Walking

Ephesians 4:1-9 is the second major section of this epistle. Here Paul explains the responsibilities of the believer to act according to the will and Word of God. Sitting is but one dimension of the Christian life. Once we have learned to sit in Christ—to know who we are in Him because of the great work that He has done—we must learn to walk.

Our lives are not static, but dynamic, filled with life and movement. We all live in time and sequence. Every morning we get out of bed and determine to act: to do things, to accomplish goals, and, hopefully, live a fruitful life...one day, one moment, one decision, one action at a time. As Christians, we are saved and sanctified, but we must live through Mondays, Tuesdays, Wednesdays, Thursdays, and Fridays.

The same Bible that tells us "It is...not as a result of works, that no one should boast" also says:

"Walk in a manner worthy of the calling with which you have been called."

"Lay aside the old self...and put on the new self."

"Do not let the sun go down on your anger."

"Let no unwholesome word proceed from your mouth."

"Let all bitterness...be put away from you."

(Eph. 2:9; 4:1,22,24,26,29,31)

The Bible calls us to action... responsible action.

Through the centuries, Christians have waged a theological war that continues today. One side says to the other, "You're into works. All your efforts are an attempt to gain that which only Christ can give you." The other side responds, "You're irresponsible. You're not taking care of day-to-day business."

We need to stop arguing and realize that both positions are true; they just reflect two dimensions of the Christian life. There is nothing we can do to gain the gifts of forgiveness and salvation. There is nothing we can add to the works of Christ on the Cross. He has done what He has done, and we can only accept it or reject it. We cannot gain admission or acceptance on the basis of our efforts. We cannot make God's work more complete. We can only sit with Him.

But once we have accepted our position in Christ, we must walk in a manner worthy of the foundation which was laid by Christ. It is our responsibility to do everything in our power to serve Him; to walk in obedience, to walk in the light, to walk in the Spirit. Though we sit in the heavenly places because of what God has done, we must act and behave in a responsible manner worthy of our position in Christ. We must walk.

## Standing

This brings us to Ephesians 6:10-20, the "stand" section of Ephesians. It is at this point that we are instructed "finally" to take our stand against the enemy. We will never be able to stand confidently and resolutely against the powers of darkness if we are not first secure in our salvation. Unless we are *seated* and relaxed before the Lord, knowing who we are in Christ and trusting in the wonderful grace of God which is able to keep us from falling; and unless we are *walking* with a clean conscience; we will not be able to *stand* against evil powers.

Unfortunately, we often have it backwards: We stand and contend to keep our salvation, and we are seated and relaxed when it comes to the powers of darkness. If you're never quite sure whether you're saved or not, bombard your mind and heart with passages of Scripture that establish all God has done—like Ephesians 1-3. Only when God's truth sinks in and finds an immovable home in your life will you be able to sit and relax in your salvation.

On the other hand, if you never think about the need to walk responsibly on a daily basis, you need to dwell on Ephesians 3-4 and other Scriptures that emphasize your responsibility to make proper choices according to God's will.

God calls us to "lay aside the old self" and to "put on the new self." This is as easy to understand as putting on and taking off our clothes. It is responsible action. We're all used to choosing and acting appropriately in mundane matters. We brush our teeth regularly and we change the oil in the car when needed. Putting on the new self is another daily responsibility, a right choice. It is not works; it is simply our proper response to God and all that He has done for us.

We cannot work for our salvation in any way. It is a free gift of God. But once we've taken hold of this gift, we must keep a clean conscience before God. First John 3:21, 22 reads, "If our heart does not condemn us, we have confidence before God; because we keep His commandments and do the things that are pleasing in His sight." Then and only then are we ready to stand before the enemy.

Until you are absolutely relaxed and confident of your salvation; until you "walk in a manner worthy of the calling with which you have been called" (taking care of business on a daily basis); you will never be able to consistently stand before the enemy. But when you are, you are in a position to stand.

It sounds like an acrobatic wonder, but we must stand, sit, and walk at the same time. Only then are we prepared to move on and defeat the powers of darkness. We can "finally, be strong in the Lord, and in the strength of His might." Then we are ready for spiritual warfare.

# CHAPTER THREE

# Knowing Your Enemy

*For our struggle is not against flesh and blood, but against the rulers, against the powers, against the world-forces of this darkness, against the spiritual forces of wickedness in the heavenly places (Eph. 6:12).*

Every good soldier goes into battle well prepared. Not only is he appropriately armed to defeat his enemy, but he knows what to expect when he arrives on the battlefield. More importantly, he understands the nature of his enemy and of the war in which he is engaged.

In Ephesians 6:12, the King James Version uses the term "wrestle" in place of "struggle." In Paul's day, wrestling was a popular sport, so Paul used it as an analogy of spiritual warfare. There are some important similarities between the sport of wrestling and spiritual warfare.

Unlike most sports, wrestling does not allow any time to relax or catch your breath. From the moment each round begins, wrestling demands constant concentration. Every thought must be focused and every muscle ready. To let up in concentration, even for a moment, is to ensure the opponent's victory, or at least the loss of advantage.

Like wrestling, spiritual warfare is constant. If I could impress Christians with only one thing, it would be that our battle is absolutely constant. The war is being waged 24 hours a day, seven days a week, 52 weeks a year. Satan does not take Saturday nights or Monday mornings off, and he never calls in sick. He is relentless in his attempts to thwart the work of God in us and through us.

When I say that the battle is constant, I do not mean that we must struggle to maintain that which God has done. We don't need to struggle to achieve salvation. The grace of God has placed us in that position. We stand not *for* our salvation but *because* of it.

As mentioned before, most spiritual warfare is won in our awareness of the work of the enemy. It is not a matter of struggling all the time, but a matter of being aware that the battle is going on every minute of our lives.

## We Can't Live in Disneyland

Perhaps Satan's greatest advantage over the children of God is his consistency, as opposed to our inconsistency. Christians are notoriously inconsistent. We fluctuate between periods of intense devotion to God and periods of self-imposed alienation from Him.

The devil has seen our inconsistency before. He has heard people declare, "I'm going to really get to know the Lord. I'm going to change the world and do great things for God." But Satan is not very impressed with our momentary surges of consecration. He knows how many Christians on the first of January commit themselves to regular prayer and Bible reading, only to lose heart before mid-February. During our times of strength and serious devotion to God, the devil can afford to wait patiently until we let down our guard. Satan will wait for weeks, months, and years, if necessary.

How often have you heard Christians make these kinds of statements?

"I don't know about things right now."

"I'm confused."

"My leaders have failed me; my friends have failed me; God has failed me."

"I'm really going through it right now."

"I just need to step back for a while, take some time to get my head together."

I wish we lived in a different world—a Disneyland-world where we could take time off from life and from the battle between righteousness and unrighteousness. But we can't. We can never take a vacation from Christianity. We cannot put God or Satan on hold. We can never say, "God understands if I just coast a while. He knows my tragedy, my circumstances, my hurt. He will give me a little time to lick my wounds." God does indeed understand our struggle, pain, and grief, but He intends for us to live in victory not in defeat. He offers us grace to be more than conquerors. And though *He* understands, there is one who will *never* make allowances for us—Satan.

## Just How Bad is He?

Wouldn't it be nice if the devil would leave us alone when we are going through rough times? I wish he would, but I must inform you, he does not. He always fights dirty. Satan sees our down times as his opportunities. True to his nature, he strikes with vile determination when we are weakest. We can expect no less than this from the enemy. We must not underestimate how evil Satan is, nor how terrible his intentions toward us are.

Satan is relentless in his attacks because he utterly hates us. He desires our complete destruction. There is no goodness in him at all. He is absolutely void of virtue and compassion. This is his nature and he is not going to change.

Think of the most evil, grotesque things people do to one another. Think of the ovens in Nazi concentration camps, or lamp shades made of human skin. Think how many horrible ways men have conceived of torturing and murdering one another...tying people atop a pile of logs and watching them burn, or binding arms and legs to four horses, which gallop in four directions, tearing the victim apart. Remember the Gulag Archipelago, or the bombing of black churches in the South, killing little girls in their Sunday best. Think how some parents can rape a four-month-old baby or pour scalding water on their children. Men do unspeakable things to one another—obscene, monstrous acts of violence. Every day in prisons around the world, eyes and fingernails are plucked out and people are forced to eat their own excrement. In witches' covens, babies are killed and eaten. I met some people in a refugee camp in Thailand who told me terrible stories of soldiers slicing open pregnant women and little unborn babies falling out into the mud as the rest of the family stood watching in anguished disbelief.

We recoil in horror from these terrible things that men do to one another. For the most part, we are sheltered from the terror of these realities. But these things have all been spawned by our enemy. Satan is far worse than anything real or imagined. We must have a revelation of our enemy. Just as we need a divine revelation of God's goodness, mercy, and love, so we must also have a revelation of Satan's evil and destructive power.

The devil has no sense of fair play. He has no mercy. When we are down, he kicks us. Like a shark, he moves in for the kill when he smells blood. He is full of hatred and thrives on torment. When the tragedies come—when you've failed at school, when you've lost your job, when your husband or wife has cheated on you, when your family has been killed in a car crash—that's when the devil pulls out all the stops and pursues you with savage vigor.

It is only human to be devastated when tragedy strikes us, and to experience emotional trauma. But during these times, we must also remain aware, watching for the attack of the enemy.

Satan marks our weakness, whether it be lust, doubt, or depression. He waits patiently for a perfect opportunity, and then plants seeds of destruction in our lives. While he watches them take root, we notice it too late or not at all.

Our responsibility is to recognize the enemy's consistency and surprise him by searching for areas of weakness that have caused us to fail in the past. If you've ever had a car accident on a particular stretch of highway or at a particular intersection, you cannot pass that place again without being intensely aware of the dangers there. You drive far more carefully past that point, if nowhere else. In the same way, we can be strong and overcome where we have failed in the past.

**"Satan Hates You and Has a Horrible Plan for Your Life."**

"The thief comes only to steal, and kill, and destroy; I came that they might have life, and might have it abundantly" (John 10:10).

This verse describes the nature and activities of the devil. This is what Satan does: he steals, kills, and destroys.

He is a thief who wants to rob us of all he can. He wants to steal our health and another year of life. He wants to steal our productivity, our relationships, our joy, our peace, and our faith.

How many times have you said, "What a terrible day I've had." "What a total loss this week has been." "What an unproductive month!" This is exactly what the enemy wants. He wants to plunder our lives one day at a time. We bolster the enemy's thievery by falling into his "bad day" formula. We must be alert and aware. We can't let him have our days. To do so is slow suicide, for our lives are just a sum of our days. When circumstances threaten us we must say, "Satan, I'm not going to allow you to have this day or this moment, and I'm not going to allow you to rob me of my joy."

Satan is also a killer. He loves to kill. Anything that has to do with death is fully supported and encouraged by him. He is the major influence behind statements like, "I wish I'd never been born," and "I wish I were dead." He would love to drive us all to suicide and murder.

Many people, even Christians, have entertained the idea of ending it all, but every suicidal thought is from the cruel, killer heart of Satan. I'm not trying to blame everything on him, but suicide is the devil's work. It is his nature to destroy us; it is not natural for us to desire self-destruction. God created man with survival as his strongest instinct. Suicide is suggested by the powers of darkness to needy, desperate hearts.

When the devil can't guarantee our immediate self-destruction, he will influence us toward a slower form of suicide—some self-destructive escape from life. The most obvious forms of slow suicide are drugs and alcohol. Whenever we say, "I can't handle life, so I'm going to drop out with this," we're on the road to suicide. It is the same principle and the same spirit. The particular form can vary, and even seem innocent: It could be an addiction to food, sex, television, or shopping. But if we're using something to avoid life, to hide from reality, it is suicide—it is death.

Satan also wants to destroy us with sin. He tempts us toward sin with the seductive promise of fulfillment. For instance, if we are unfulfilled in our marriage, we believe we can find fulfillment in the arms of another. However, the enemy has never intended to give us fulfillment. When we go outside of truth and righteousness for fulfillment, we enter the domain of the powers of darkness. Our participation in sin gives the powers of darkness permission and opportunity to work in our lives. We become co-workers with Satan in his goal to ruin our lives.

Satan is real. His evil nature, his intentions, and his participation in our affairs are real. When we enter his territory, we are making friends with a remorseless thief, a diabolic destroyer, and a monstrous murderer.

His full intention is to destroy our minds, our bodies, our character, our reputations, and our relationships. He yearns for the eradication of all that is righteous and good. And yet there are many people who feel that they can play around with sin—that they can dabble with the powers of darkness. "God understands," they say. "He'll forgive me." The issue is not whether God understands and forgives. We can't dally with the most perverse, most heinous, most murderous creature in the universe and escape. The choice is ours. When it comes to sin, either we stand *against* the enemy or we stand *with* him.

## Harmless Hokum or Mortal Danger?

*There shall not be found among you anyone who makes his son or daughter pass through the fire, one who uses divination, one who practices witchcraft, or one who interprets omens, or a sorcerer, or one who casts a spell, or a medium, or a spiritist, or one who calls up the dead. For whoever does these things is detestable to the Lord... (Deut. 18:10-12).*

Satan's lure to destruction is very seductive and equally deceitful. His plans are elaborate and extend to every living being. Sometimes his plans are hidden, while at other times they are blatant, as in the case of the New Age movement.

Throughout the last two decades, the growth and widespread acceptance of the occult has been incredible. In one way or another, these trends affect most of us. Every morning over coffee, millions flip to the horoscope section of the daily newspaper to find out what their day will be like. If you're more wealthy, you can have a personal astrological chart made, or perhaps hire a channeler. On the shelves of every department store, in desk drawers, and in the toy chests of millions of children are tarot cards, Ouija boards, Dungeons and Dragons games, and comic books with demonic characters. Palms are read at county fairs, and people glare into tea cups for a glimpse of the future.

The concept behind some of these things is simply that there are good days and bad days, and we can discover which is which. After John Lennon was murdered in New York, some so-called experts said that if John had only checked he would have known that the day of his murder was a bad day for him. They say he shouldn't have even left the house.

Many think that these are just innocent practices, or mere nonsense. I'm sure many horoscope columns are simply the wild guesses of people willing to entertain the curious. There is nothing demonic about groundless predictions in the morning paper. Yet to God they are an abomination—not because of their content but because people are choosing to open their lives to the plans of Satan.

Satan really does have a plan for our lives. Christians need to be aware of this—*aware*, not alarmed. We need to know that if we consult a supernatural source for information, we open ourselves to powers of darkness. The danger is in our choice— our willingness to go to someone other than God for a seemingly harmless glimpse of the future. That glimpse can open us to a plan for our demise that really does exist in Satan's mind.

In the Old Testament, participation in occultic activities was absolutely forbidden. Those caught in witchcraft, fortune-telling, or spiritualistic exercises were taken outside the city and stoned to death. God is serious in His condemnation of such things.

Instead of memorizing a list of forbidden activities, we should know this one principle: Any supernatural information or activity is either from God or from Satan. If it's from God, it comes via the Holy Spirit, in the name of Jesus, and according to the Word of God. Other supernatural occurrences are an abomination to God. They are an abomination because even the seemingly good things of Satan lead to destruction and bondage. They are wrong because *God* wants to direct, guide, and inform us. Whatever guides us is our god, and we are commanded to have no other gods before Him (Ex. 20:3).

## Who is Best at Telling the Unknown?

It's a shame that the psychics and the occultists have reintroduced the great understanding of the supernatural to the world, when the Church has known about it all along. Unfortunately, the Church is still pawing through theology books, wondering whether God is still doing supernatural things today, while the psychics are telling the police departments where to find the bodies I'm waiting for the day when the police will call the church and say, "Will you people pray to God for information?"

The main reason God does not want us consulting other supernatural sources is because He wants to be our only source of supernatural activity. The living God loves us and wants to be our guide. He has promised in Psalm 32, "I will guide you." In John 10, Jesus said, "My sheep hear My voice." The Bible is full of the promises of God for guidance, help, and correction. Why don't we just go to God? He has His plans for us. He will give us all the supernatural information and activity we could ever want in the fulfilling of those plans. Even if we don't understand at the time, and even if we have trouble hearing His voice once in awhile, we can still trust His character. We can still believe that He will direct our steps. He has an impeccable record. He has never hurt nor failed anyone. He has never been anything other than faithful, just, and kind. Surely we can place our trust in Him.

## Ups and Downs

We all have natural ebbs and flows, both emotional and physiological. The female monthly cycle is one example. These ups and downs are not demonic in nature. The enemy, however, seeks to exploit these natural cycles. We must be on guard. We do not have to allow these cycles or the devil to ruin any day.

When David woke up in the mornings, he was sometimes worried and depressed. But David would say to his soul, "Don't be discouraged. Don't be upset. Expect God to act!" (Ps. 42:11 LB). David continually encouraged himself in the Lord.

God does not expect us to be emotionally up all the time. It's normal to feel down at times, to be depressed, or sad. I used to think that when I became spiritually mature I would have no more ups and downs. Then I saw one of those heart monitors on TV and noticed that ups and downs are a sign of life. When it becomes a flat line it means you're dead! Christian maturity doesn't mean we have no down times; Christian maturity is learning to handle our ups and downs. We must remember that the enemy often attacks when we're vulnerable. We need to learn how to encourage ourselves and one another.

## Spiritual Radar

Spiritual warfare demands alertness—a constant vigilance toward the enemy's activities. How many times have you heard the admonition, "Don't think or talk about the devil. Just keep your eyes on the Lord"? Now, it is not possible to keep our eyes literally on the Lord. That statement means we should stay attentive to God. He can work in and through us because He loves us and is keeping us by His power. It means to be aware of God, remembering who He is and what He is doing.

There is nothing wrong with that advice, but it's about time the Body of Christ adopted another one: "Keep your eyes on the devil." For most of us, that is an uneasy prospect. Somehow, we have believed that if our eyes are on the devil, they can't be on God. But we can all come to a place where we are constantly aware of the living God, while being aware of what the enemy is doing, too.

If I were in the middle of a battle, with shells exploding around me, I might approach the colonel and say, "I see there is a war going on. Who are you fighting? How many of them are there? What are their objectives? What are their movements? What kind of ammunition are they using?" What if he were to answer, "Well, we don't worry about the enemy. We don't like to discuss him much. We don't know where he is or what he's doing. We're just shooting our guns and lobbing our hand grenades. Why, today we've shot off 17,000 rounds. Isn't that exciting? Aren't we doing well?"

The absurdity of a war fought with such ignorance is clear. Yet I've often heard such an approach to spiritual warfare from well-meaning Christians attempting to protect themselves from the powers of darkness. But ignorance of the enemy will not protect us. We must keep our eyes on him! On the other hand, if we keep our eyes on the devil, but not on God, we are also in trouble. We *must* keep our eyes on God, and without fear, keep our eyes on the enemy as well. We must know where he is and what he is doing.

This alertness is much like radar. In order to have any value at all, radar must be constant. If the dish stops turning for any predictable period—evenings or weekends, Christmas, holidays, a monthly maintenance check, or when the operator isn't feeling well—the radar system is useless. If we spend six months on the alert against the powers of darkness, only to drop our guard for a day, we can be sure the enemy will strike that day. He anticipates our failure to maintain a constant vigilance. He plans for and takes full advantage of our lapses.

The mere presence of radar is often enough to discourage the attack of enemy planes. In the same way, our constant awareness can deter Satan in his attempts to hinder us. When the devil comes into view on our radar screen, red lights and buzzers should go off within us, preparing us for attack and often averting the attack altogether.

# CHAPTER FOUR

# Three Battlegrounds

Bridges. Roads. Airfields. Television and radio stations. In any war, strategic areas are heavily fortified in order to keep them from the enemy. Whoever holds the key places will probably win the battle. In our lives, there are three strategic areas which we must fortify against attack: the mind, the heart, and the mouth. Like critical military positions, we must fight to protect them until our last breath.

## The Mind: The First Strategic Area

Every thought that enters our minds has three possible sources. First, thoughts can originate within ourselves. God created us with the ability to produce thoughts independent of any other source. They are *our* thoughts. Secondly, thoughts can come from God. God can speak into our minds. Whether we call it revelation, guidance, the voice of God, or the gift of the word of knowledge, He does speak directly into our minds. The third source is the enemy. The forces of darkness also speak to us. Unfortunately, many Christians listen to the enemy, are influenced by him, and suffer the consequences.

Some may ask how the devil could speak to our minds. He is not omnipresent, so what does it mean when the Bible tells us to "Resist the devil and he will flee from you" (James 4:7)? When the Scriptures speak of Satan or the devil, sometimes they are referring to his evil empire rather than the individual, Lucifer himself. The devil couldn't possibly be in hundreds of thousands of places at the same time, tempting people and putting suggestions in their minds. His fallen angels (the Bible doesn't tell us how many there are) are the ones carrying out Satan's orders. In all probability, most of us wouldn't merit Lucifer's personal attention. When God's Word tells us to resist the devil, I believe it is telling us to resist spirit beings belonging to Lucifer. For the sake of simplicity, I will often refer to Satan in this book in the generic sense, when I mean any one or all of his fallen host.

While the forces of darkness cannot read our minds—only God can do that (Ps. 7:9)—they can put suggestions there. Remember when Peter argued with Jesus when He said it was necessary for Him to die and rise again after three days? Jesus responded to Peter, "Get behind me, Satan!" (Matt. 16:23). Jesus wasn't saying that Peter had suddenly become demon-possessed; evidently Peter was speaking out the thought Satan had just whispered into his mind.

Most spiritual warfare takes place in the human mind. It involves recognizing when a thought is not righteous, or when it does not agree with God's truth. Not all evil thoughts are from Satan, but he will exploit them and add to them.

Once, while driving home from a meeting, I realized that my mind was filled with arguments and criticism about the other spiritual leaders with whom I had met. It suddenly occurred to me that I didn't really intend to be critical or unloving toward these people. Yet my mind was overflowing with negative thoughts against my friends. I had to catch myself and recognize that these thoughts were from the enemy.

The enemy loves to discredit people and destroy relationships. It is Satan's delight to fill our minds with accusations against our husbands or wives, our leaders, our friends, or people from a particular country or city, or against God himself. He is "the father of lies" (John 8:44) and the "accuser of our brethren" (Rev. 12:10).

### Afraid of the Dark

God is a creator. He created everything in this universe from nothing. He did not have a stockpile of raw materials. Nothing existed until it was imagined in the mind of God. We who are created in the image of God are also creators. God gave us active imaginations. Although God created the world we live in, we have added things like concrete, lights, automobiles, microchips, sculptures, and symphonies. We have a phenomenal God-given ability to create with our minds.

This wonderful ability can also be a target for the powers of darkness. The devil regularly fuels our imagination with falsehoods and unrighteousness. We worry and are fearful of what we imagine will happen, even though those bad things rarely happen. Many are frightened of the dark. It isn't literal fear of darkness. Fear of the dark comes when sight is hindered and the imagination pictures terrible things—things that are not real.

When we give the devil access, he is more than happy to supply the images to pervert our creativity. For instance, Ted Bundy was a mass murderer responsible for 18 killings; he was executed in Florida in 1989. Before his death, he told Dr. James Dobson how he had been influenced by all the violent pornographic material he read.

God never intended our imaginations to be abused through unholy, evil input. He gave us imagination for faith. Faith is imagining what God has spoken as though it were already complete. When we see it done in our minds, we have faith. That's what the Bible means when it says, "Faith is the substance..." (Heb. 11:1 KJV).

> *For though we walk in the flesh, we do not war after the flesh: For the weapons of our warfare are not carnal, but mighty through God to the pulling down of strong holds; casting down imaginations, and every high thing that exalteth itself against the knowledge of God, and bringing into captivity every thought to the obedience of Christ (II Cor. 10:3-5 KJV).*

I have heard people use the term "strongholds" to refer to humanism, Islam, communism, and other religions and institutions. However, in II Corinthians, "strongholds" does not refer to massive, complex systems, human or demonic. Here it refers to the strongholds of the mind. These strongholds are castles in the air built up in our minds through wrong thinking—through unbelieving, depressed, fearful, and negative thinking.

Two mental strongholds are extremely common today among Christians and non-Christians alike: thoughts of inferiority, and thoughts of condemnation.

Inferior thoughts constantly tell us, "You're not big enough. You're not smart enough. You don't look good. You're not really making it in life. You're worthless." These barbs keep us competing with and envying others.

Satan also accuses, "You're not pleasing God. You are not spiritual enough. You do not read your Bible enough. You're not close to God." These thoughts make us feel as if we can never break through into the fresh air and sunshine of God's approval. Some Christians live every day of their lives in dreary condemnation.

These two strongholds must be cast down through spiritual warfare, as we refuse them and instead accept what God says about us in the Bible.

## A Mental Sentry

Thoughts can be like food that enters our mouths. We are not aware of each morsel. We may not stop to think about each bite, but when we get a mouthful of rotten fruit, we automatically spit it out. In the same way, dealing with thoughts and imaginations can become automatic.

Every military post has guards. They stand quietly at their posts until they hear a rustling in the bushes. Then they immediately ask: "Who goes there?" and are prepared to evict any intruder. We too need to post a guard at the gate of our minds to check the credentials of every thought and every imagination, ready to cast down that which is not true, not righteous, or not of God. If it doesn't belong, out it goes. This is spiritual warfare: being alert to every thought.

The Bible says, "As he thinks within himself, so he is" (Prov. 23:7). One of the devil's greatest schemes is to nullify the effectiveness of Christians who are genuinely saved. Even if they go to heaven when they die, Satan will be happy to blunt their lives while on earth. He disables them, stealing their days, months, and years by influencing them to think wrongly. Unfortunately, Satan has successfully neutralized thousands of potential victors this way.

## The Heart: The Second Strategic Battleground

*Watch over your heart with all diligence, for from it flow the springs of life (Proverbs 4:23).*

When the Bible refers to "the heart," it means many things. In regard to spiritual warfare, I am taking two of the Bible meanings—the attitudes and the emotions.

The Bible speaks of protecting important parts of our anatomy with the armor of God. Both physically and spiritually, the head and the heart are most vital and vulnerable. An arm or leg can be lost in battle, but a wound to the head or heart brings almost certain death. In a spiritual sense, our heads and hearts are equally vulnerable, and demand equal protection.

We Christians stand firmly against sins of action, but we do not guard our attitudes with equal diligence. If we were to find out that a preacher we admired was an adulterer, homosexual, or thief, we would be outraged. We would take immediate action, refuse to attend his meetings, and do everything we could to remove him from the office of ministry. But if instead we knew that a dynamic speaker was rebellious, independent, contentious, proud, arrogant, and angry most of the time, we might very well dismiss it. We may shrug, "It's nice to find someone who isn't afraid to be human—just like us."

However, the Bible's standard is not so tolerant. Ephesians 4:26-27 says, "Do not let the sun go down on your anger, and do not give the devil an opportunity (or place)." Anger is not the only wrong attitude we can have, of course. But we can see from this verse and those following it that any wrong attitude allowed to fester can give the devil opportunity to attack. And remember, in this epistle Paul was writing to one of the more mature churches of the New Testament! Unlike the Galatians or Corinthians, the Ephesians were not a problem case. Theirs was a church full of relatively mature, Spirit-filled, wholly devoted Christians. Yet Paul felt it necessary to warn them not to give the devil a place. He didn't say that they were doing that, but that they *could*.

What was possible for the Ephesians is likely for us. It is more than a possibility. Unfortunately, the areas which we relinquish most readily are our attitudes and the words and actions that they cause.

### Brushing Your Teeth and Dealing with Attitudes

Too often we allow wrong attitudes to take root and manifest themselves unchecked. To keep the enemy from our hearts, we must immediately deal with wrong attitudes that surface. "Do not let the sun go down on your anger" doesn't tell us we won't be angry; it just says to deal with anger.

We can't think that all our bad attitudes disappeared when we were saved. The Bible is clear about our daily responsibility to manage life, to make choices, and to correct wrong attitudes.

We take showers and brush our teeth every day. We would never think to say, "I'm just not into works, so if God wants me dressed today, He'll get me dressed," or, "If God wants my teeth cleaned, He'll brush them." We know that these small matters are our responsibility, and we consistently do them. Whether we are tired, depressed, or confused, we always put on our clothes before we leave the house.

We should be just as responsible when it comes to dealing with wrong attitudes. If we say, "I don't have to be responsible for my actions and my attitudes today," or, "I don't have to repent, be humble, smile, or be encouraging when I don't feel like it," it is as silly as saying, "February is a hard month for me; I think I'll wait until March to have a shower."

Putting off the old self and putting on the new self (Eph. 4:22-24) means taking daily responsibility to deal with our attitudes. These responsibilities cannot be ignored because we're new Christians, or because we're burnt out, because we don't understand, or for any other reason (Eph. 4, Col. 3:8).

Living responsibly and consistently is very important because the powers of darkness can ride on our attitudes. If we remain in pride and rebellion, there is no guarantee, even from God, that we are protected from the powers of darkness. If we tolerate bitterness over months or years, we are providing a place for the enemy (Matt. 18:34, 35). We are not talking here about the fact that we have been justified by faith and stand in God's grace, but about shutting any doors to the enemy.

People who have allowed a "root of bitterness" to spring up in their lives are easy to recognize (Heb. 12:14, 15). Everything bothers them and they become angry, critical people. Everyone they touch is defiled. They can switch circumstances, husbands, wives, or organizations, but nothing will keep them from bumping up against others who bother them.

When a root of bitterness surfaces, we must deal with it immediately. It is relatively easy to uproot a tree when it is a small shoot. But when the tree is full-grown, uprooting it becomes a monumental task. The roots have spread so far and are so large that it can take tractors, dynamite, and a lot of digging and chopping. This is exactly what it is like when we allow bitterness and other bad attitudes to linger. It pays to respond quickly. When we notice that we are bitter toward someone, we must not let the sun go down before we have dealt with our bitterness. We must pull it out of our lives before it begins to spread and go deeper.

If we tolerate bitterness, rebellion, independence, pride, or unbelief, we cannot live in victory. I often hear Christians say, "Well, I guess I'm just a little bit rebellious. I'm not a 'yes man,' you know. I like to question everything." This might sound harmless or even colorful if there were no devil. But there are powers who desire our destruction, and these attitudes are a slippery slide downward to spiritual defeat.

Many I counsel are being kicked around by the devil—even though he is a defeated foe. They've been saved for years and are on their way to heaven, but the enemy is wreaking havoc with their lives, sometimes daily. They have problems in their personalities, marriages, and relationships because they are giving place to the enemy through wrong attitudes that they refuse to change. This is not the exception among Christians; it is as common as breakfast.

Jesus won a total victory by shedding His blood on the Cross for us. But we will not experience that victory in our daily walk if we do not deal with wrong attitudes in our heart. God does not hold us responsible for that which we do not know. However, when He reveals wrong attitudes, we have to deal with them quickly and completely.

## Choosing Humility as a Way of Life

*Humble yourselves, therefore, under the mighty hand of God, that He may exalt you at the proper time, casting all your anxiety upon Him, because He cares for you. Be of sober spirit, be on the alert. Your adversary, the devil, prowls about like a roaring lion, seeking someone to devour. But resist him, firm in your faith, knowing that the same experiences of suffering are being accomplished by your brethren who are in the world (I Peter 5:6-9).*

It is just as important to deal with negative emotions as with wrong attitudes. Emotions are not wrong. God has emotions and He endowed us with them. They are an important component of life. Without emotions, we would live a gray, colorless existence. The devil, however, loves to inspire negative emotions. He influences people's emotions to a tremendous degree.

First Peter 5:6-9 gives us the way to deal with emotions and attitudes. The first injunction is to *humble* ourselves. What does it mean to humble ourselves? It is choosing to be known for who we are—no more than we are, and no less. And how often should we humble ourselves? Well, how often do we take a shower? As often as we need to. Humbling ourselves whenever we need to is the key to living a perfect life.

Christian perfection is still a controversial subject in the Church today. Some say, "No one is perfect." But Jesus was perfect, and He lives in the heart and mind of every believer. Biblical perfection is not perfection in behavior. No one can live without occasionally doing something wrong. The Bible speaks of perfection in motive and commitment. Biblical perfection is commitment to truth. If we violate truth, we must be committed to putting it right immediately by humbling ourselves before God and others, and repenting.

Biblical perfection does not mean that we will never be resentful or angry. It does mean that when we recognize these things in our lives, we will deal with them immediately by humbling ourselves. Humbling ourselves must be a way of life. It is as simple as saying: "I'm sorry, I was proud. Will you please forgive me?" It is dealing with whatever surfaces when it surfaces.

We have a promise from God that if we humble ourselves, He will exalt us. However, if we exalt ourselves, God has also promised to abase us (Matt. 23:12). If we do not humble ourselves when we should, we are in effect exalting ourselves. It is far easier to choose humility as a way of life. A genuine humbling is always followed by an exaltation. God keeps His promises, and we should never fear humility.

## Nullify Satan's Three Kingpins

In dealing with attitudes and emotions, we are also instructed not to worry—we are to cast all our anxiety upon Him. Worry indicates fear and unbelief. We cannot trust God and worry at the same time. To worry is to doubt God's willingness and His ability to take care of us.

Of the hundreds of admonitions in the Bible, these two—to humble ourselves and not to worry—are pivotal to spiritual warfare.

So many of us are impressed with Satan's massive and complex kingdom. The occult, witchcraft, eastern religions and philosophies, humanism, pornography, drugs, murder, and every devisable evil are orchestrated by the powers of darkness. This horrendous domain of darkness is influencing the entire world, and can be overwhelming to the Christian who is not even more impressed with God and His Kingdom.

Within this enormous and complex structure of evil are three kingpins that hold it all together. These kingpins are the basis for everything that Satan does. If we don't allow these things in our lives, we have effectively disarmed Satan and nullified his undertakings in our lives. These three are pride, unbelief, and fear. Everything that Satan does, his entire kingdom and his nature, emanate from pride, unbelief, and fear. These things should never be tolerated in the lives of Christians.

We deal with pride by humbling ourselves, and we deal with unbelief and fear by casting our anxieties on God.

### Being Sober, Yet Able to Smile

Peter continues imploring us in I Peter 5:8 to "Be of sober spirit." Being sober is often equated with not being drunk. Another misinterpretation is to equate soberness with a particular facial expression.

I grew up going to church with a gentleman who thought it was improper to smile on Sundays. He believed Sunday was a holy day, not a day for levity, but a day to be sober. He would sometimes join us for Sunday dinner. We children watched to see if he would ever forget and grin, but he never violated his conscience.

When it comes to spiritual warfare, being sober means to be constantly aware. It is not allowing yourself to be under the influence of anything that would hinder your consciousness of that which is around you.

If we were in the front lines of a battle, where bullets and mortars were flying around our heads, we could find protection in a trench or foxhole. The bullets would fly over the trench, and we could have relative peace behind the sandbags. We could generally relax as long as we remembered where we were. If we forgot where we were for even a second, we would be apt to raise our heads out of the trench and be killed.

So long as we are sober—always aware of where we are and of potential threats—we can enjoy life to its fullest and be confident that the Holy Spirit is keeping us from danger. Christians can have more fun in life than anyone. Life is to be enjoyed. But in every situation, every social gathering, every form of entertainment, and in every conversation, we must remember where we are. We are on the front lines of a real battle, where there is no warm-up or pretend time. It's the real thing.

The next step given in I Peter 5 is to "Be on the alert." We must keep our eyes open—ever vigilant—in order to recognize the works of the devil.

Peter then tells us to be humble, to not worry, to be sober and alert, because "Your adversary, the devil, prowls about like a roaring lion, seeking someone to devour." We often forget our real adversary. It is not a leader, a cantankerous co-worker, or our mother-in-law. Our adversary is the devil. He is the adversary of each individual Christian. We tend to think of the powers of darkness as a nebulous evil force that filters into everyone's life but doesn't attack personally. Yet Satan's most successful assault on Christians is against the individual, not against the Church as a whole.

## Don't Be Afraid of the Roar

This roaring lion seeks to devour God's children, but cannot because of the keeping power of God. The devil knows this, and although he cannot truly devour Christians, he intimidates by his roar alone. This often blunts any effectiveness an individual might have had.

A lion's roar, the power in his jaws, and the sharpness of his claws are frightening. It is easy to respond emotionally when confronted by a mighty roar and the anticipation of death. But if we react to the devil's roar and move away from obedience to God, we can allow the devil to defeat us.

Satan roars and we jump. He roars and we get angry. He roars and we lust. He roars and we get depressed. He roars and we become rebellious. Are we being guided by the roar of the lion or by God?

We change jobs because we need more money. We marry because we're lonely. We move because we want a bigger house to make room for more things. We leave churches because we get angry and fed up, or because we doubt that it will ever improve. Where is the voice of God in these decisions? If we make decisions out of emotion alone, God is not our guide. We are being guided by the roar of the lion, moved by our anger, fear, and pride from a place of protection to a place where the devil can and will devour us. If we look around, we will see the empty pews or vacant posts of those who were led by the roar of the lion.

Satan is a fast learner who quickly discerns our weaknesses. It is his nature to tempt and attack where we are weakest. He will continue to do the one thing that works, over and over again for the rest of our lives. He will tell us that when he roars, we must respond. He'll tell us that's what we are and we can't do anything about it. But these are lies. No bondage is greater than Christ's ability to free us.

God wants to be our guide. He loves us and knows what's best for us. He gave us emotions, and wants us to be emotionally fulfilled. We are to laugh and sing, to have fun and excitement. We are also to grieve, cry, and mourn. Our lives are intended to have emotional balance. But we are not to make life's decisions on the basis of these emotions. We must be led by God—not by our emotions nor the roar of the lion.

There is a humanistic philosophy that says, "If it feels good, do it." This is a selfish, anti-God, anti-Christian statement. What we feel should have no bearing on our choices. However, what we do choose will have a tremendous effect on how we feel. We are to obey the truth no matter how we feel. If we obey God, eventually good feelings will follow.

God wants us all to be able to plant our feet and say with total determination, "I will not move, no matter how I feel or what I want. I don't care how depressed, humiliated, broke, hurt, disappointed, or disillusioned I get; I'm not moving from this spot until God clearly directs me to move."

God must know, and we must know that no matter what happens, we will only respond to Him. Even when we are in the depths of despair, when we have been unjustly treated, when others have failed us, and when all our emotions are crying out for us to run or to quit, we must stand and wait for God. He will not fail us. We must say "no" to ourselves and "yes" to God. This is spiritual maturity. The devil will not let up until he sees that determination in us.

# The Mouth: The Third Crucial Area

So often we who are supposed to be encouragers of the brethren and proclaimers of truth allow our mouths to become tools of destruction in the hands of the devil. Many deep hurts in the lives of those I've counseled can be traced back to comments made to or about them. They carry wounds as real as physical ones, caused by spoken words.

Words are amazing tools that can bring life or death. Words of the mouth combined with heart attitudes bring "spirit power." A sermon or message that is anointed and brings revelation has spirit power. Those words and the righteous heart of the speaker give the Holy Spirit opportunity to open minds and hearts to His truth. Through Spirit-anointed words come the power to change lives.

Our words can be vehicles of the Holy Spirit for truth, righteousness, and life, or vehicles of Satan for deception, accusation, and death. Words, like music, are a medium. A medium is amoral: neither good nor evil.

The fact that words have power is not new to many Christians. We believe that if someone on the other side of the country is sick, a group of people thousands of miles away can agree together in prayer and affect the physical body of the sick person. We believe in the power of prayer. If words have no power, and God is going to do what He is going to do, then we might as well give up praying. But words do have power with God, if we pray according to His will, agreeing with what He has promised.

### Where Did That Sentence Come From?

If we can release supernatural power to help someone who is sick on the other side of the country, what kind of power is released when we gather to complain and criticize? When words flow from a selfish or judgmental heart, we tend to think we aren't really doing any harm. But words are powerful, and our mouths are either wellsprings of life or of death. "Death and life are in the power of the tongue, and those who love it will eat its fruit" (Prov. 18:21). David prayed, "Set a guard, O Lord, over my mouth; keep watch over the door of my lips" (Ps. 141:3). David's prayer needs to be our prayer.

The importance of guarding our mouths is demonstrated in the story of Job. Not that we are to keep silent and bottle up all our pain and anger—in the midst of incredible suffering, Job was anything but quiet. Yet the Bible declares Job did not charge God foolishly, neither did he sin with his lips (Job 1:22; 2:10 KJV). This is an amazing statement, for Job certainly did not keep silent. He shouted questions at God. He screamed, "I don't understand! You are just, so why is this happening to me?" And even, "God, you're going to get a bad reputation from this!"

However, in all his frankness, Job never crossed that line. In the words of my friend, Tom Hallas, Job was never "disloyal to the character of God." Satan gained no access into his life because Job never sinned with his lips.

Could God say the same about us—that we have never sinned with our lips? When things are pressing in on us, when we are confused or suffering, are we loyal to the character of God? Are we careful with our lips?

## Disguising an Ugly Progression

There are many ways of sinning with our mouths, and Satan loves to inspire our words. It often happens when we gather with friends. It starts with someone making an innocent *comment* about someone not present. The comments become *observations,* then the observations turn into *concerns.* Concerns become *criticisms*, and criticisms becomes *accusations.* Oh, we may disguise the ugly progression. Our harsh words can be couched in "words of love":

"We really need to pray for John because...."

"I'm just sharing this so you'll know what to pray for...."

"I'm not judging her, BUT...."

"He's such a wonderful leader, BUT...."

James 3:10 says, "From the same mouth come both blessing and cursing." We can actually release supernatural blessing from our mouths, or we can aid the enemy's attack on people.

Our mouths can also tear down what God is trying to build among us. Almost every group has someone who is "anointed in unbelief." This person sees faults and impossibilities in every project and every concern. He can influence the whole group, uttering negatives until everyone believes "it will never work." Spreading negative reports, as the ten spies did in Numbers chapter 13, makes God angry because it hinders what He would have His people do.

There is power in our mouths. What we speak out has spirit power: negative or positive. The words which spring from our hearts can defile us and others. We must watch over our mouths. It takes discipline—the discipline to simply keep our lips tightly pressed together when our hearts are burning to say what shouldn't be said. "But the things that proceed out of the mouth come from the heart, and those defile the man" (Matt. 15:18).

If we can consistently watch over our minds, hearts, and mouths, we will deny the devil access to our lives and truly experience victory. We will be ready to go on the offensive.

# CHAPTER FIVE

## Steps to Spiritual Fitness

*Let the weak say, I am strong (Joel 3:10 KJV).*

We have already seen that spiritual warfare is like wrestling in that it demands constant alertness. There are other similarities. Wrestling demands physical, mental, and emotional conditioning. In fact, wrestling requires a greater degree of physical fitness than most sports. Likewise, spiritual warfare also requires a high level of spiritual fitness.

*Be strong in the Lord, and in the strength of His might (Eph. 6:10).*

In discussing spiritual warfare, the Bible commands us simply to "be strong." It does not say that we can only become strong after years of being a Christian. Nor does it suggest that we are weaklings who can never become strong. We shortchange ourselves far too often by denying who we are and what God has done for us. We obtain our theology from hymns like, "I am weak, but Thou art strong." The Word of God says "Let the weak say, I am strong," and, "Be strong." We deny this when we who are strong in the Lord declare our weakness.

A prominent government official recently stated publicly that Jesus told us to do some wonderful things, but of course no one is able to live them out. Many believe that what the Bible says is not possible—that the Bible's goals are unreachable.

This attitude is in contradiction with the truth. It is in direct opposition to the Word of God, which says we are new creations in Jesus Christ. Yet how many Christians will confess that they are strong, humble, or holy?

### Is God Playing Cruel Games?

Would God ask us to do something that cannot be done? Would God ever toss us three shoes and tell us to put one on each foot? I am shocked at how many actually hold this view of Christianity. This view is like a carrot hung in front of a donkey. He is never able to taste the carrot, but he will constantly trot on while it dangles just out of reach. Is God playing cruel games with us, or are we able to do what He has asked us to do—to live as He instructs us to live?

Christianity is not just a belief or a confession, but a life. There is no biblical principle to which we cannot adhere, no command which we cannot obey, and no promise beyond our grasp. When the Bible says, "Be strong," we can be strong. When the Bible says "Be humble," we can be humble. When the Bible says "Be holy," we can be holy.

Not that we can do this alone. Pride says, "I am strong in myself." People who have this pride quickly discover the hard way that they need God. He is our strength. All that we are, all that we have, and all that we can do is because of Him.

We are in a spiritual battle, and if we do not know that we can be strong, we will live in constant defeat. What a tragedy to never be what God tells us we can be, because we think it is impossible. We are strong. This is not boastful. This is not pride. This is humility—agreeing with God's truth. In Christ, we are strong.

# Spiritual Conditioning

Any athlete must maintain physical conditioning through jogging, exercise, and weight training. He may be strong, but he must maintain his strength. For spiritual warfare, it is also important to stay in condition.

There are a number of things we Christians can do to maintain our strength. The first is to talk to and listen to God. Not that routine, ritualistic prayers will give us strength. Prayers may or may not strengthen us, but talking to God always will.

We have moved away from open, honest conversation with God. Prayers can be little more than words, but intimate conversation with the living God brings us life and makes us strong. We must enter into the presence of God and talk with Him, aware that He is concerned and listening. Then we must be equally willing to listen to Him. Strength comes from being in His presence.

Secondly, we should meditate on the Word of God. Like prayer, this must not be a mere religious exercise. Reading the Bible may or may not strengthen us, but meditating on it always will. Like all of us, I have read several chapters of the Bible, only to realize that my mind was elsewhere. I hadn't absorbed a single grain of truth. It's easy to walk away from our regular Bible reading with a sense that we've done what is required. But what have we accomplished if we haven't meditated, understood, believed, and embraced God's Word? We've done nothing more than a religious activity.

Some of us have been exposed to thousands of sermons and Bible verses. If any of them have made a difference in our lives, it is only because we have taken the time to consider them at length and to explore the implications. Verses we only read have no real significance in our lives.

I play a little game that has helped me meditate on God's Word. Every time I hear a sermon or read the Bible, I pretend someone points a finger at me and demands, "Tell me what you have just learned." This forces me to reflect and sometimes return to the Bible, to meditate as well as to read.

## Openness Makes Us Strong

Another thing that we must do to be strengthened is to have fellowship. Like Bible reading, this too can be nothing more than religious activity. We have all gone to church, shaken hands, patted backs, and dispensed smiles, hugs, and greetings without ever being strengthened. The whole idea behind fellowship is not just to have a meeting, but to promote relationship with those with whom we have the most in common: our brothers and sisters in Christ.

Just going to church may or may not strengthen us, but true fellowship always will. Fellowship begins with openness and honesty. Relating to one another in humility strengthens us. Pride, independence, and shutting others out of our lives will never strengthen us, no matter how many meetings we attend. We can be in the midst of people and still be hiding. But when we lower our defenses in the right place, at the right time, in the right amount, with the right people, we are able to join in true fellowship. This is openness with accountability.

> *But encourage (exhort) one another day after day,*
> *as long as it is still called "Today," lest any one of you*
> *be hardened by the deceitfulness of sin (Heb. 3:13).*

Genuine fellowship includes exhortation. We have a responsibility to exhort and keep one another from hardness of heart. We need to be involved and concerned, encouraging each other to greater faith, love, and obedience on a daily basis. This requires commitment to one another and a willingness to consider others' welfare as an essential part of our walk with God (I Thess. 2:11; 5:11).

Maybe church needs to be less ceremony, and more like a support group. God never intended us to live out our Christianity alone, without the support of others. We are part of God's family. We have brothers and sisters who love us, and want to support us in our struggles and trials. And we must do the same for them.

### Praying in the Spirit

> *These are the ones who cause divisions, worldly-*
> *minded, devoid of the Spirit. But you, beloved, building*
> *yourselves up on your most holy faith; praying in the*
> *Holy Spirit....(Jude 19, 20).*

Another means of spiritual conditioning is praying in the Spirit —speaking in tongues. "One who speaks in a tongue edifies himself..." (I Cor. 14:4). Whether or not one believes in the speaking of tongues, the Bible remains clear about one of the many things it does for the believer: Praying in the Holy Spirit builds us up and strengthens the inner being.

We are also strengthened when we worship—not that we only worship for what it can do for us. We worship for God's sake. However, true worship will always strengthen us; singing, shouting, and raising our hands may or may not. We too often confuse worship, which is of the heart, with action that may be little more than religious ritual. True worship is boldly coming before the throne of God with a clear conscience and bowing down before Him. It is genuine contact with God.

## Even Babies Can Be Strong

These are some of the things that will help us maintain our strength. Why do we need to be strong? Because there is a devil who preys upon the weak and upon those who think they are weak. We need to be strong, because the Bible tells us to be strong. We need to be strong, because our strength is an essential part of our relationship with God. To be strong is to know God, to love God, to talk with Him, hear from Him, worship Him, and confidently stand with Him in victory.

We have unintentionally taught each other that we are weak and that new, baby Christians are weak. This idea is not found in the Bible. New Christians are no weaker than old Christians. The term "baby Christian" or "new Christian" should denote only a level of maturity or accumulated experience, not impotence and helplessness.

There are many things we don't know. We are still growing and continually needing to be transformed into the likeness of Christ. Our characters are continually being perfected. But in Him, we are not weak. We are strong in His strength and we must stand confidently in strength against the enemy. "We have gained access by faith into this grace in which we now stand" (Rom. 5:2 NIV).

## Learn the "Holds"

Another thing that is true about wrestling, and also true about our battle, is that we need to know the holds. Wrestling matches are won not only on the basis of strength, but also as a direct result of knowledge. If a champion wrestler in my weight class were to challenge me to a wrestling match, he would undoubtedly win because of his knowledge of wrestling holds. When he first began wrestling, an important part of his training was acquiring knowledge. He could not stop in the middle of a match and refer to a wrestling book. His knowledge of wrestling moves and holds had to become second nature to him beforehand.

This is equally true of spiritual warfare. We are indeed strong, but there are some basic things that we must know. We must know the spiritual warfare holds.

We have seen that spiritual warfare and wrestling are both constant. This has troubled some in sessions where I have taught on spiritual warfare. When I say that spiritual warfare is constant and no one is exempt, I see a common reaction. Some have said,"Wait a minute, Dean! I have been taught the rest of faith. I have been taught not to struggle and strive. I have been taught, 'Don't wrestle, just nestle,' and 'The battle is not yours, but the Lord's.'" Some people see a contradiction, but there is no real discrepancy here. We can rest even in constant battle. The key is knowing the holds.

If a champion wrestler were indeed to wrestle me, he probably wouldn't have to remove his coat. His match with me would be quick and painless (for him) and would drain none of his strength. He would dispense with me in seconds, without even working up a sweat. He would need no shower afterward and would feel no threat to his wrestling crown. His victory would be assured before the match began, and would require little thought or effort on his part. He could be at rest before and after, if not during the bout.

## Resting During Battle

It is true that the battle is constant. If we do not recognize this, we could live in continual defeat. Christians need to know that there is never a minute of our lives when the battle is not on. If, however, we walk in strength and know the holds, the battle will not be a major impediment. We can walk through each day fully assured, able to deal with each crisis, circumstance, or attack from the enemy as it arises. It is constant, but we can rest in our strength, dependent upon God.

The rest of faith does not mean spiritual inactivity, that nothing will happen, and that we need not respond. "The battle is not yours but God's" does not mean that we can passively spend our lives watching TV while God battles the powers of darkness on our behalf. In II Chronicles 20, "The battle is not yours but God's," is followed by "Tomorrow go down." We are responsible to fight the devil in God's strength, and if we are strong and know the holds, it is not an enormous burden but a routine discipline—one in which we can rest.

*For to this end also I wrote...in order that no advantage be taken of us by Satan; for we are not ignorant of his schemes (II Cor. 2:9-11).*

Paul said, "For we are not ignorant of his (the devil's) schemes." The problem is that too many of us are ignorant. We have been taught to be ignorant of the schemes of the devil—to ignore him and to wrongly interpret the "rest of faith" as passivity.

We can learn to recognize Satan's schemes. In every situation, we can pick out that which is of the devil and deal with it. We can recognize his schemes to destroy our marriages, hinder our relationships, or draw us into depression. Recognizing the schemes of the devil is knowing the holds. It begins with knowing the enemy's holds, and ends with a counterhold that will quickly end the battle.

When we recognize the schemes of the enemy, they fail. Just recognizing them brings us victory. He preys on our ignorance and our weakness, but fails when confronted by our strength and knowledge of his schemes.

### God's Secrets to Help Us Win

*Yet we do speak wisdom among those who are mature; a wisdom, however, not of this age, nor of the rulers of this age, who are passing away; but we speak God's wisdom in a mystery, the hidden wisdom, which God predestined before the ages to our glory; the wisdom which none of the rulers of this age has understood; for if they had understood it, they would not have crucified the Lord of glory (I Cor. 2:6-8).*

There is a wisdom which is hidden from the powers of darkness, but available to us if we are humble before God. This wisdom, the writer of Hebrews says, is for those who are mature. Hebrews 5:14 says: "The mature, who because of practice have their senses trained to discern good and evil." The secret wisdom of God is for those who are learning to recognize the schemes of the devil. We can train ourselves to recognize the schemes of the enemy—to be able to determine what is from the devil and what is from God. God's wisdom will help us discern and recognize the works of the enemy in our lives and in the world around us. If we wait on God, we will know the holds. We will recognize the plots of the enemy against us. We can respond immediately, saying, "I know what the devil is trying to draw me into here. I won't do it. I will not give way to depression. I will not join in criticism. I will not get angry at my wife. I will not get involved in this wrong relationship." We can see his schemes coming and stand our ground. If we know the holds, we can counter them, and spiritual warfare will become a routine that is as comfortable as taking a daily shower.

## Don't Point Your Guns the Wrong Way

*For our struggle is not against flesh and blood, but against the rulers, against the powers, against the world-forces of this darkness, against the spiritual forces of wickedness in the heavenly places (Eph. 6:12).*

Almost every sermon on Ephesians 6:12 focuses on what our battle is and who it is against. Our battle is against rulers, powers, world forces, and spiritual forces. However, an equally important truth from this verse is *what our battle is not* and *who it is not against*. Our battle is not against flesh and blood. We tend to forget this. For centuries the Christian church has failed to follow the most important directive in spiritual warfare—never battle against flesh and blood.

I often meet people who want nothing to do with spiritual warfare. They think it is spooky and strange to stand against the devil or rebuke the enemy. People may be reluctant to fight Satan, but we are all experts when it comes to battling people. Everyone has, at some time, defended his or her position in anger, or criticized, rebuked, offended, or condemned others. There are few who have not battled flesh and blood.

The only problem is, the Bible forbids fighting flesh and blood. It tells us that we should never, under any circumstance, at any time, for any reason, fight against flesh and blood.

The reason a defeated devil has consistently beaten a so-called victorious Church is because we are always fighting one another. We have wasted multiplied hours criticizing other denominations, and preaching sermons and writing books against each other, and have lost the real battle. It has never been, and never will be, a Christian activity to write books and articles or make speeches against other Christians. We get into savage theological controversies that neither side will ever win. The devil must be laughing, since he's the only victor.

What's worse, we are not battling the one who is really the cause of these problems. While we are fighting our leaders because they aren't doing what we want, while we are fighting our brothers because they believe differently, and while we are fighting our co-workers, Satan is running rampant on the earth. And it's our fault.

## Being Right, But Missing God

This is the history of the Church. The Crusades, the Inquisition, burnings at the stake, persecutions, and church splits have all been done in the name of God, Jesus Christ, and spiritual warfare. We must understand that we are never to fight people. We can win the argument, and still lose. We can be right, and yet wrong in our attitude. Even if we have the right doctrine, if we damage people in defense of it, we give the enemy entrance. It's okay to fight issues, but not the people behind the issues. We can never win if we battle other human beings.

It may be hard to swallow, but the Pharisees were right. They understood the Scriptures completely. Their doctrinal statements were in order. They knew how to be good Jews. They were the Bible believers of their day, committed to uncompromising obedience to the Word of God. Yet they were so proud of their righteousness that they missed God in human form. Jesus walked before them, spoke to them, and rebuked them, but they could not see Him because they were too proud of being right. Jesus stood against this attitude, attributing it to the enemy (John 8:44). The Pharisees crucified God Himself while defending godliness and rightness.

All of our struggles with one another, our fleshly battles throughout history until today, have only strengthened Satan's grip on the earth, on the lost, and on the people of God. Our pride has brought us into a battle in which any participation at all means defeat. We must not battle against flesh and blood. If we fight, people we cannot fight the enemy.

There is a cliche which says, "He's so heavenly-minded, he's no earthly good." It is true. Some people can be so overly spiritual that they cannot be practical or responsible. But perhaps it's time for a new cliche: "We're so earthly-minded, we're no heavenly good."

There are two realms: the earthly and the heavenly. The earthly is that which we can see and touch—the physical realm. The heavenly realm is the unseen world, where the real battle is taking place. Every hour of every day, while we sleep, eat lunch, watch TV, and kiss our wives, a constant battle is being waged in heavenly places, a battle that has been going on for centuries. It started before we were born and will continue after we die. The battle is fought over the affairs of men on the earth. It is between the forces of darkness and the forces of light.

We can be so earthly-minded, fighting our fight in the earthly realm, that we are of no value in the heavenly battle. We fire our cannons in the wrong realm. If we are not fighting in heavenly places, we will fight in earthly ones. If we are not doing battle with the powers of darkness, we will fight people instead. There is something within us that gets incensed at injustice, something that rises up in protest of wrongdoing. If we do not take that into the heavenly places, resist the enemy, and pray for a change, we will fight people. We should fight issues in society, but not people. Fighting people never advances the Kingdom of God, no matter how right the issues. God's Kingdom is advanced through God and His response to our prayers, and through our Spirit-led actions.

## Can God Really Handle It?

The words of a popular hymn say it better than I:

> *Oh, what peace we often forfeit, oh what needless pain we bear, all because we do not carry everything to God in prayer.*

If we truly believe that the Holy Spirit is able to speak into the hearts of people and has a far greater level of influence than we do, shouldn't we first take everything, every concern, every observation to Him? Unfortunately, we often come to God after we have failed in our attempts and have left a trail of bruised and wounded hearts. And all the time, we were convinced we were right.

Is our first impulse to pray, or do we believe that we are more capable, more persuasive than the Holy Spirit? Can we deal with people better than God? Can we straighten out our kids, correct our husbands and wives, discipline our followers, rebuke our leaders, and remedy every conflict more easily than the Spirit of God? Are we certain that God is as interested and capable as we are? Any action on our part to deal with people prior to immediate, heartfelt prayer and intercession stems from immense pride. We believe we can handle things better than He can.

God loves people far more than we do, and He is far more capable than we are, exerting incomparable influence on people's hearts. If we truly believe these things, wouldn't we be constantly in prayer for one another?

# Five Things to Remember

### 1. We should pray before we act.

Even in situations where we have responsibility as pastors, leaders, or parents, we should always pray first. As a parent, I have the responsibility to discipline and correct my children, but I need to pray before I act. As leaders, we sometimes need to reprove, but we must give God the first opportunity through prayer. It's not that we do nothing and God does everything. We pray first, giving God a chance to minister into the situation and maintain the relationships. God will either act directly into that situation, or give us wisdom in how to respond.

## 2. We should resist the enemy and take authority over him.

The problem is not the person, but the powers of darkness who take advantage of every situation, multiply conflict, hinder reconciliation, and destroy relationships. We should face every situation with a willful verbal stand against the devil. We should say, "Satan, I rebuke you. You will not have my marriage, my kids, my friend, my leader. I stand against you and bind you in the name of Jesus." We can stop the enemy from hindering God's work in the lives of those around us.

## 3. Rather than fighting flesh and blood when we are rebuked, we can assess honestly whether there is any truth to it.

Every rebuke, every criticism, and every accusation should be humbly considered. They may be wholly or partly true.

When we consider the possibility that we might be wrong, we are open to the ministry of others in our lives. This is humility. This is spiritual warfare.

Pride has crippled the Church for centuries: "I am right and others are wrong. I know; you don't." We are usually more wrong than we would like to admit. But even when we are right, and really do know the truth, we must be open and willing to examine the content of what others say to us. Though some of what they say will be false, we need not be defensive, and should definitely not fight people. If there is truth in what they say, it becomes an opportunity for us to repent, make restitution, and become more like Jesus.

## 4. We must never lose faith or fall under condemnation.

People's words, whether right or wrong, should not cause us to waver in our faith in God's Word, our confidence in our salvation, or in our strength and maturity. When others disagree with us, we can become emotionally crippled. The criticism is so harsh that we melt before our accusers and agree with whatever they say. If the criticism comes from leaders, there is a tendency to simply submit to their claims. We doubt ourselves. We doubt what we have always believed to be true, and can even doubt God. We say, "They must be right. I guess I'm wrong. I'm always wrong. I don't know what to believe." We lose faith.

Simply take the word they say is from God to Him in prayer. If in humility and openness we do all that we should before God, and then He does not confirm to us that their word is from Him, at that point we can reject their words with confidence. We can leave them with God. We never need to lose confidence, but can remain strong in our faith.

### 5. We should maintain relationships at all costs.

Proverbs 18:19 says, "A brother offended is harder to be won than a strong city, and contentions are like the bars of a castle." If we fight people, we are not serious about spiritual warfare. If we allow relationships to falter, doctrines to divide us, and people problems to flourish in our lives, we are not building up the Kingdom of God, nor tearing down the kingdom of Satan. We are actually hindering the Kingdom of God and aiding the kingdom of darkness.

### The Right Way to Be Angry

We need to use what God has given us in the right place for the right battle against the right foe. Why has He equipped us with the ability to criticize, be angry, and argue? It is so that we can be angry about sin and the devil, releasing our anger in prayer and standing against the enemy. Anger can be sin when we selfishly direct it toward other people in pride. But remember: God gets angry, but never sins. His anger is never selfishly motivated, and never comes out of pride. He gets angry for the right reasons and uses His anger the right way. We, on the other hand, get angry when our pride is hurt, or when hampered in our selfish intents.

If we could only redirect our combat toward the powers of darkness; if we could harness the emotions and energy spent fighting one another and direct them toward the real enemy; we would see widespread change. We would see the total collapse of a satanic empire that we have allowed to exist too long. If each of us were determined never to fight another human being as long as we lived, Satan would tremble. We would do to him what we have been doing to one another for centuries. We would realize the truth: Our battle is not against flesh and blood.

# CHAPTER SIX

## The Invisible Terrain

It was a muggy day in Horse Camp, a squatter's village in Papua New Guinea. I was sitting with my interpreter in a shanty made of scrap tin and wood, trying to explain to a lady the reality of the spirit world.

"Oh, you mean the ———?" she said. The interpreter explained she had used the Kiwai word for demon. "Oh, yes," she nodded. "There were three in my house this morning. Here, I drew pictures of them." She handed me a paper with hideous half-human, half-animal looking beings on it.

I learned that day in Horse Camp, and in many other places since then in Asia, the Pacific, and in Africa, that I did not have to convince people of the reality of the spirit world. They live with it on a daily basis, often seeing evil spirits with the naked eye. And now, even in America, we have celebrities and public figures hearing spirit guides and seeking out channelers whose voices change as they tell of ancient things.

However, for the most part, those in Western countries view the unseen world as fanciful. Westerners place it in the same category as Superman, Mickey Mouse, and the Hobbit. We may think it is real, but not as real as the world we can touch, see, smell, buy, and sell. Instead of seen and unseen, we think of these two realms as real and unreal.

Even as Christians, we may admit that this realm exists but see little connection with it. We think we really can't know the unseen—that there is a dividing wall that keeps us from a see-through, spooky, Casper-the-Ghost world. Our feet are on solid ground, and the other world seems less substantial. The unseen is identified with people who are superstitious, mystical, or weird.

However, it is essential that we become well acquainted with the invisible realm. Because our battle is in heavenly places, we must not let earthly concerns keep us from walking in awareness. The hidden world affects every facet of our lives.

## The Unseen World Is Actually Less Fragile

The unseen world is just as substantial as the world we see. In fact, it is even more permanent and less fragile. If a nuclear device were to explode directly over where you work or live, the building, furnishings, wood, concrete, and all those solid things around you would be completely vaporized. However, the invisible world the Bible talks about would remain unscathed. It existed before concrete and wood, and will continue to exist long after they are gone.

The Apostle Peter realized this. He said, "But the day of the Lord will come like a thief, in which the heavens will pass away with a roar and the elements will be destroyed with intense heat, and the earth and its works will be burned up. Since all these things are to be destroyed in this way, what sort of people ought you to be in holy conduct and godliness?" (II Peter 3:10, 11).

More time and energy need to be invested in the unseen world. I believe it would be right and mature for all of us to ask ourselves two important questions every day:

*"How are my attitudes, activities, and words affecting the unseen world today?"* and,

*"How is the unseen world affecting me at this moment?"*

If we would just ask these two questions, we would greatly increase our effectiveness as spiritual warriors. They are not easy to ask because we tend to ignore what we cannot see. But we as Christians have an absolute reference point and guide to the realm of the spirit—the Bible. It is a record of events in the unseen world. You cannot read it without being introduced to the heavenly places.

We could compare the existence of the unseen world to that of the microscopic world. Though our senses are not equipped to see the billions of tiny microscopic animals around us, they are there. Other examples come to mind: Music and color pictures that we cannot see are floating around us at all times. It is only with a radio or television that we can capture them. There are worlds within worlds. Those which we cannot see, hear, or touch are as real as those we can. If someone today were to deny the existence of radio waves, gases, or germs because they are invisible, we would think they were uninformed or just plain crazy.

The principal inhabitants of the unseen realm are angels. We need to meditate on the reality of this truth. There are angels all around us. As I travel in ministry to various churches and groups, I hear about experiences people have had with demons, but not enough about the great angelic allies in our battle.

The reality of angels needs to be commonly accepted, even taken for granted. For instance, if I said there are many chairs in my house, you wouldn't consider me mystical. You could come visit me and see them. It would not be difficult for you to agree with me. But if I said there are angels all around you right now, you would be less certain, less willing to acknowledge them. As a Christian you might say, "Well, I think so. I sure hope so. There probably are." But we need to come to the point where we are absolutely convinced of their reality. We need to be able to acknowledge their existence as easily as we can chairs in a room.

## Can We Trust the Bible As Much As Our Eyes?

We are so willing to believe in the existence of chairs as opposed to angels because we can see them and touch them. We rely on our eyes and other senses to perceive things as they are. However, our eyes are not always reliable. We have all been in very dark places where we imagine shadows and dark objects to be something they are not. People see mirages in the desert. Sleepy eyes see things move that never did.

Do we believe that the Bible is at least as reliable as our senses? Our eyes are usually reliable. The Bible, on the other hand, is always reliable. If I am convinced when I see chairs that they are real, how much more should I be convinced when the Bible says, "The angel of the Lord encamps around those who fear Him" (Ps. 34:7)?

Some may ask if this is real, or just David's poetic metaphor for God's protection. It could be a metaphor if this were the only mention of angels in the Bible. But other passages make it clear that angels are a fact of life, sent by God, surrounding us and active on our behalf. The Bible is as clear in its declaration of angels and their role as it is on salvation, the atonement, the deity of Christ, and many other points on which we stake our spiritual survival. We must acknowledge the unseen world with the same certainty as every other Bible truth.

Why are angels important to us? Because when we experienced salvation, we entered into the realm of angels. "But you have come to Mount Zion and to the city of the living God, the heavenly Jerusalem, and to myriads of angels" (Heb. 12:22). Salvation is a package of blessings. We have been forgiven of our sins. We have become new creatures. The old has passed away. We have a heavenly home. We are sons and daughters of the living God. And we are surrounded by myriads of angels every minute of our lives. How many of us go through any given day secure in that fact? Angels are all around us as surely and as concretely as the ground we stand on. It is not mystical, unnatural, or strange. It is real.

## But What Do Angels Do All Day?

What are these countless concealed beings doing all around us? Are they sitting on clouds, playing harps, and flapping their wings? Not according to the Bible. Hebrews 1:14 says, "Are they not all ministering spirits, sent out to render service for the sake of those who will inherit salvation?" They are busy serving those who will inherit salvation—that is, every Christian.

How many times have you thanked God for the ministry of angels on your behalf? Few of us ever do. It is a hideous sin to grumble, complain, and be unthankful. Think of the extent to which God has provided for us. How can we ever be ungrateful and complain, knowing that God has deployed angels who constantly watch over us? We often measure God's provision and concern for us by what we see and have, giving no thought to His tremendous kindness and generosity in the heavenly realm.

> *For He will give His angels charge concerning you, to guard you in all your ways. They will bear you up in their hands, lest you strike your foot against a stone (Ps. 91:11, 12).*

I have often wondered if God might show us a video replay of our lives when we get to heaven. It would be interesting to see our lives—not just from the vantage point of the seen world, but the unseen as well. I imagine we would see ourselves walking through life with angels on all sides, protecting us from harm, shielding us from attack, and aiding us in our efforts to serve God. Besides this, the Holy Spirit would also be there helping and influencing us. I am absolutely convinced that such a replay would reveal we were saved from disaster thousands of times. Would such a replay also show we were grateful, thankful, and content? Or would we be constantly griping while the Holy Spirit and God's angels were doing everything they could to help us?

Angels are part of our lives, and with thankful hearts we should be constantly aware of them. There is even evidence in the Scriptures of guardian angels: "See that you do not despise one of these little ones, for I say to you, that their angels in heaven continually behold the face of My Father who is in heaven" (Matt. 18:10). The term "little ones" does not just refer to children, but to those who are dependent upon God—God's children. The word "their" indicates an assignment to a specific person. It would seem that we all have angels specifically designated by God to watch over us. They are constantly beholding the face of God, anticipating further direction.

## A Revealing Story

> *And when [Peter] knocked at the door of the gate, a servant-girl named Rhoda came to answer. And when she recognized Peter's voice, because of her joy she did not open the gate, but ran in and announced that Peter*

*was standing in front of the gate. And they said to her,*
*"You are out of your mind!" But she kept insisting that*
*it was so. And they kept saying, "It is his angel" (Acts*
*12:13-15).*

One of my favorite considerations about angels comes from this story of Peter's imprisonment. Peter was thrown in jail for preaching the Gospel. The Church went to prayer. What happened next is significant: An angel came into Peter's prison cell.

Remember, this is not fantasy. It is not Saturday morning cartoons, nor the Twilight Zone. This actually happened to another human being right here on this solid earth.

How did the angel get into the prison? How did he remove Peter's shackles? And how did he get himself and Peter out of the prison cell? We don't know, but we do know that what happened was a result of the unseen world going into action in the seen world. Equally important is the fact that through the prayers of the Church, the seen world affected the unseen world and brought about Peter's release. This single biblical account should, at the very least, provoke us to pray in every situation.

A second thing in this story is noteworthy regarding the unseen realm. Notice what they said to themselves to explain what they couldn't believe: "It is his angel."

This indicates two things: First, those in the Early Church were aware of the unseen world. "It is his angel" was their first reaction. Secondly, it indicates that they knew individuals had assigned angels. The first Christians, under the leadership of the apostles, were not mystics or involved in bizarre, super-spiritual practices. They are an example to us of a balanced, both-feet-on-the-ground approach to the Christian life. And they assumed that angels were part of their lives.

### Is the Old Testament a Comic Book?

The Old Testament is full of stories and evidence of the unseen world. However, we often distance ourselves from its historical events. Although we would never admit it as Christians, we perceive an element of fantasy in the Old Testament. The miraculous stories are far from our experience, and the Bible heroes have the feel of comic book characters. Even God in the Old Testament seems to be an exaggeration of the God we have come to believe in—the God of the Old Testament seems more powerful, more active in the affairs of men. We see our present world as a greater reality, while the Old Testament world seems partially illusory.

However, the events of the Bible are factual. If our lives do not reflect these facts, we have distanced ourselves from truth and reality.

A story from the life of Elisha also sheds light on angels:

*Now when the attendant of the man of God [Elisha] had risen early and gone out, behold, an army with horses and chariots was circling the city. And his servant said to him, "Alas my master! What shall we do?" So he answered, "Do not fear, for those who are with us are more than those who are with them." Then Elisha prayed and said, "O Lord, I pray open his eyes, that he may see." And the Lord opened the servant's eyes, and he saw; and behold, the mountain was full of horses and chariots of fire all around Elisha (II Kings 6:15-17).*

Elisha was a prophet as well as the leader of the "school of the prophets." Their school found themselves in a city completely surrounded by an enemy army. One of the students, seeing the army, ran to tell Elisha.

Elisha's reaction was not one of fear, but of confidence. Without raising an eyebrow, Elisha simply said, "Don't let these circumstances distress you, for those who are with us are more than those who are with them."

At this point, the young man could have thought Elisha had lost it. He looked around him...no one was in the house but them, and there were only enemies outside. But Elisha wasn't crazy. He was more in touch with reality than his young friend. He was aware of the unseen world.

Elisha prayed, asking God to *open the young man's eyes*. Suddenly, he saw the angelic army. God did not simply fill this man's head with a dream. He did not create some symbolic projection. God did something to the optical abilities of his eyes so that he was able to see what was actually there. The young man saw that "the mountain was full of horses and chariots of fire all around." I can imagine his surprise, excitement, maybe even fear. This young man saw a world completely new to him. The unseen world became as real as the world of flesh and blood he had always known.

### But What Did Elisha See?

Some say that Elisha had faith because his physical eyes could see what others couldn't. But the Bible doesn't say that. Perhaps Elisha never did see with his eyes what the young student did. He was just aware of the unseen world around him. It was only the young man who needed to be convinced.

Heightened awareness of the unseen realm would correct many problems. I have met countless people who are not doing the work of God because they are taken up with pessimism, casualties of their own words, victims of their circumstances or of other people. But if we trust God, we need never be victims. One of the great ways to overcome daily is to become aware of our tremendous unseen allies in this battle. We must live in this knowledge 24 hours a day, as assured of it as we are of what we see, hear, smell, touch, and taste.

Elisha lived in that realm and we can too. When we are faced with difficult circumstances, overwhelming odds, and ruthless foes, we need not be victims. Neither should we spout negative words that drag us and others down in defeat. We need only know that we have our foe outnumbered. "Those who are with us are more than those who are with them."

## Three Kinds of Angels

When the Bible speaks of angels, it indicates three distinct roles they assume.

### 1. Warrior Angels

The first role is that of warrior angels: angels who fight. Daniel 10 and Revelation 12 talk about an archangel who is the chief (or prince) of these angels. His name is Michael, and he is associated with the angelic armies of God.

How often do we think about angels fighting? Until the publishing of Frank Peretti's book, *This Present Darkness*, many did not consider this biblical reality. Even now, many Christians don't consider it at all. We might think it strange and medieval, but the Bible is clear. As surely as Jesus died on the Cross and we have salvation through Him, angels are doing battle in the unseen world at this moment.

Daniel 10 gives us a peek into the unseen realm. Daniel prayed for three weeks without receiving an answer. This alone is remarkable. Most of us would have given up after twenty minutes. Daniel could have quit, but he prayed and fasted for 21 days, and may have continued beyond that had not a wonderful thing happened. An angel came to him.

> *Then he said to me, "Do not be afraid, Daniel, for from the first day that you set your heart on understanding this and on humbling yourself before your God, your words were heard, and I have come in response to your words. But the prince of the kingdom of Persia was withstanding me for twenty-one days; then behold, Michael, one of the chief princes, came to help me, for I had been left there with the kings of Persia"* (Dan. 10:12-13).

Later the angel says, "But I shall now return to fight against the prince of Persia" (Dan. 10:20).

This story should convince us of some exciting truths: First, *our prayers are heard from the first day*. No matter how discouraged we feel, and no matter how long we wait for an answer, our prayers are heard.

Also, we learn from Daniel's story that *our prayers move God to deploy angels on our behalf*. We never pray to angels, but to God, who sends them out in direct response to our prayers. Our prayers reach the heavenly realm, which responds back to us into the earthly realm.

If we have prayed at all this week, angels are in action as a result. Our prayers are not just words that tickle God's ears. Our prayers dispatch warrior angels to battle for us and for Christ's purposes.

Furthermore, we learn from Daniel's account that *angels fight*. We don't know how they fight, but they do. Our prayers aid them in their battle. I'm sure they don't shoot each other with lasers or chop each other up with swords. They might exert some sort of force. Hebrews 1:7 indicates that angels are like winds. One angel could be a wind of righteousness pushing against the force of evil in another. We don't know for sure, and it isn't important that we know. But it is important to know that they do battle on our behalf, in response to our prayers.

## 2. Messenger Angels

The second category is that of messenger angels, or angels that communicate. Gabriel, who brought the message of Jesus' impending birth to Mary and who spoke to Daniel and Zacharias, seems to be the archangel or chief of the messenger angels. Throughout the Bible, angels were sent to talk with men: to inform, warn, or bring revelation.

On numerous occasions, I have met people who have seen angels and received messages from them. These modern people are no more mystical or bizarre than Daniel, Mary, Jacob, or countless others throughout history. Angels have not been removed or replaced by automation. I'm not sure why we don't all see angels. Perhaps our wise God knows that in our pride we would seek relationships with them more than with the unseen God. But He does allow many to see them. I believe it is to provide a few people with undeniable evidence of their existence and that of the unseen realm.

The Bible warns us not to seek—and certainly not to worship—angels (Gal. 1:8, Col. 2:18). If God wants us to talk to or see angels, that is His business. The important thing is to live in constant awareness that they are all around us. Jesus said, "Blessed are they who did not see, and yet believed" (John 20:29). He was speaking of people believing in Him, but the principle is the same. We should believe in the unseen world, because God declares it to be true in His Word—not because we can see it. Our lack of sight should not hinder our faith and bring doubt.

### 3. Worshiping Angels

The third activity of angels is to worship. There are angels who do nothing but worship God. The Bible tells of hosts of angels who worship God. Revelation shows us a picture of myriads upon myriads of angels proclaiming of Jesus: "Worthy is the Lamb" (Rev. 5:11, 12). Worshiping angels also sang at the birth of Christ.

## The Dark Side

There is no direct biblical account of an archangel over the worshiping angels. There is, however, a strong suggestion that Lucifer, who became Satan, was that archangel. Like Gabriel and Michael, Lucifer stood before God. "You had the seal of perfection, full of wisdom and perfect in beauty....You were the anointed cherub who covers; and I placed you there. You were on the holy mountain of God" (Ezek. 28:12, 14). He was also called a prince, giving him the same rank as Gabriel and Michael (Eph. 2:2).

Lucifer was a beautiful creature to look at. He was very wise. It would seem that he was in and of himself an instrument of worship. He had access to God, and seemed to hold an office or position unequaled in the angelic realm.

Then one day Lucifer was cast out of the presence of God and out of heaven. Why was this? What did Lucifer do that was so wrong? If they were honest, a lot of people would admit to some sympathy for the devil. Some say that God felt threatened at the prospect of Lucifer overthrowing His kingdom, and because He was bigger and stronger, He selfishly expelled poor Lucifer.

### Will Satan Be Saved?

This view of God feeling threatened by Satan is more common than we might think. But the truth is, God was not threatened, and never has been. In fact, it was the other angels who actually cast Lucifer out (Revelations 12). And Satan certainly deserves no sympathy. He has rejected total and absolute light and knowledge of God. He therefore has rejected whatever could bring him to repentance, and will not be redeemed.

Lucifer was cast out of heaven because of his own choices. If we know anything at all about the character of God, we can be sure that God was only grieved at the choices Lucifer made.

Lucifer said, "I will ascend to heaven; I will raise my throne above the stars [angels] of God, and I will sit on the mount of assembly in the recesses of the north. I will ascend above the heights of the clouds; I will make myself like the Most High" (Is. 14:13-14). In other words, Lucifer was declaring that he would be another god just like the one true God. To this day, he has not deviated from that plan.

It surprises me how many people, Christians included, think Lucifer is like another god. They believe God is the God of good and Satan is the god of evil; they are seen as equals, standing in opposition. Satan has tricked millions with this lie.

## There's Simply No Comparison

This is a heathen view of the world that places God and Satan as opposites like some Oriental *yin* and *yang*. They are not equal counterparts. Only God is God. He is the great uncreated Creator. He is eternal and infinite. He is omniscient (all-knowing), omnipotent (all-powerful), omnipresent (everywhere at all times), and sovereign (having supreme authority). Lucifer is only a fallen archangel—created, finite, and extremely limited in knowledge, ability, and space. He doesn't know everything. He can't do everything. And he can only be in one place at one time.

The Christian view of the universe describes one, incomparable Supreme Being. The concept of two beings ruling over two equal and opposing kingdoms with the victory shifting from side to side is taught in Hinduism, as well as other Eastern religions. But the forces of good and evil do not counter or balance one another. Although the Bible calls Satan the "god of this world," this only denotes a position of authority over his own deceptive system. The angels threw Lucifer out of heaven, and he became Satan, establishing his kingdom of darkness. And now, we battle him in the name and authority of Jesus.

God has never fought the devil and never will. It would be like the tiniest ant crawling up to my shoulder and shouting, "Hey buddy, want to wrestle?" How could I wrestle an insect that I can barely see? Apart from just squashing him or blowing him away with a small puff of air, how could I actually wrestle with this tiny ant? This ant, although bold and proud, would never be a threat to me or to anything I possess.

The idea of God fighting Satan is even more absurd than me wrestling an ant. God is infinitely greater in every respect. God can never fight Satan, which is precisely why we are supposed to carry out the battle in the power of God.

Equally absurd was Lucifer's attempt to be like God. Satan can never be like God. It is not possible for the created to become the uncreated. The finite can never become the infinite. God is God, and there is nothing in the universe that is remotely like Him.

## If You Think Lucifer Was Stupid...

If it was so impossible for Lucifer to become like God, why did he try? The answer can be found within each of us. How many of us have ever lived for ourselves? When we determine in our hearts to live without God, when we say, "I'm strong in and of myself, and I don't need anyone else to run my life," what we are really saying is, "I can be like the Most High. I am the most important being in the universe. I can be God."

Everyone in the human race has at some time said, "I don't need God." We think we are the focal point of the universe. We can go to the moon, build computers, cure diseases, and we think we can solve all of society's problems. We can perfect the human race, starting with ourselves. We don't need God, and we don't need religion. We're so independent and so impor-tant—until something like cancer strikes. Then we crawl like babies to the foot of God, crying for help.

What Satan did was absolutely ludicrous. Yet we, as finite, puny beings, subject to the common cold and just one breath away from rigor mortis, think we can run our own lives without God. To try to live without God is to try to be God. This is exactly the absurd and insane pride that entered Satan's heart, and sadly, we all have it.

## We've Believed Satan's Claims

- The name "Satan" has struck fear into people's hearts for centuries. The name itself has become a huge symbol of evil, resembling the god-like image he wishes to project. Even Christians are sometimes overwhelmed by ideas and pictures conjured up by the name Satan.

The word "satan" literally means "adversary," or loosely, "one who stands against or in opposition to." [1] At times, the word "Satan" is used in the Bible to refer to his forces—not just to the individual, Lucifer. The being called Satan is merely a fallen archangel who received his name because he opposed God. He is also our adversary. We must consider him to be that—no more and no less.

Satan is not alone in his kingdom of darkness. When he was cast out of heaven, he took many of the angels with him. While we do not know how many he took with him, we do know he has a limited number since he cannot create new beings. The kingdom of darkness is comprised of Satan and these demons, or evil spirits. The Bible does not make a direct connection between the fallen angels and demons. If demons are not fallen angels then we do not know where they came from. It seems reasonable that demons are fallen angels in spirit form. However, it is far more important to recognize the reality of the existence of demons than to speculate on their origin.

As we have mentioned, in most cultures throughout the world we would have no problem convincing people of demons or evil spirits. Also, increasingly in the so-called civilized world, well-educated, sophisticated people are regularly involved in activities that include demons. This is not hocus-pocus, uneducated folklore, or unfounded superstition. It is real. Every Christian must be aware of this reality, and we are only deceiving ourselves if we believe otherwise.

---

1  Buck, Emory Stevens gen. ed., *Interpreter's Dictionary of the Bible*, Nashville, Abingdon Press, 1962, p. 52

The kingdom of darkness, then, consists only of these types of beings—Satan (an individual fallen archangel) and fallen angels, numerous demons, and evil spirits. According to God's Word, that is all there is. These spirits are personalities. We are not fighting "the dark side of the force," or some other mystical, impersonal evil power or all-pervading energy. Jesus didn't confront a force of evil. He confronted evil spirits, sometimes naming them by name.

## Ghosts, UFOs, and Extraterrestrials

In the past twenty years, people have become extremely curious about ghosts, UFOs, and extraterrestrials. The Bible sheds no light on anything other than the personalities already mentioned. There is no lack of unexplained phenomena in the world today, but I believe the Bible provides all the information we need about the unseen realm. If the Bible isn't clear about it, we don't need to know. If paranormal, supernatural, or extraterrestrial phenomena exist, I suggest they are either activities of God's angels or the devil's.

Like all personalities, fallen angels think, listen, communicate, experience, act, and react. Because they are personalities and because of the biblical record concerning angels and demons, we know that they are able to interact with humans. They speak to us in our minds. (For instance, the devil put it into Judas' mind to betray Christ, according to John 13:2.) They hear what we say, watch our reactions, and make plans and strategies.

Because these evil personalities listen, we need to speak to them when we do spiritual warfare. Some may be reluctant to address the enemy. The Bible is clear, however, that we are to resist the powers of darkness (James 4:7, I Peter 5:9). How do we resist a personality? Should we wave our Bibles, grunt, close our eyes, and hold our breath? The only way I know to resist a personality, short of a fist fight, is to speak out resistance. We Christians are to address Satan and the powers of darkness directly, rebuking them, and verbally denying them access to our lives. Jesus addressed the enemy directly. Having told us that we would do greater things than He, Jesus has shown us by example that we too should address the enemy, resisting him.

In Mark 16:17, Jesus commissioned us to use His name in coming against the enemy. He didn't say He would confront them for us—He said that in His name, *we* would cast out devils."

This is enough for us to begin to win daily over Satan and his forces. But there's more...more understanding, more of the devil's present strategies we must discover and combat.

# CHAPTER SEVEN

# Satan's Hierarchy and Battle Plans

We now know who comprises the kingdom of darkness—Satan and demons. We need to consider how his kingdom operates, or to use Bible terms, to not be "ignorant of his devices" (II Cor. 2:11 KJV). If we were on a police force, we would learn to overcome a criminal by recognizing his "m.o." or *modus operandi*.

Satan's m.o. can best be described as a three-pronged assault on the world.

## Prong # 1: Satan's Hierarchy

The first prong of that assault is a hierarchy. This hierarchy is there to oversee and control events in the world. As the god of this world, Satan has far-reaching strategies. Like any hierarchy, there are different functions. Three functions of the kingdom of darkness are described in the Bible: rulers, principalities, and powers. These terms vary slightly in different versions of Scripture, but the important thing is to know the functions and combat them.

## Rulers

The Bible uses words like "thrones," "dominions," "authorities," and "rulers." These words describe offices held by spirit beings. Ruling has to do with exerting opinion or will over others. It is important to understand how the enemy gets access to the earth to exert his opinion over the will of men.

Jesus spoke in Matthew 16 of the "gates of hell." In Bible times, the leaders of a city sat at the gates to make decisions governing a town. Therefore, the modern equivalent to "gates" would not be the city limits, but City Hall—or Congress, Parliament, the Oval Office, the Kremlin, #10 Downing Street—any place where important corporate decisions are made. Satan infiltrates existing human authority structures, seeking to rule through them. And how does he do this? The same way he always has. Since the Garden of Eden, Satan has gained access to rule through the wrong, selfish choices of men and women.

When thinking of authority or governmental structures, we tend to focus only on the highest levels. But authority structures are far more extensive and layered, touching every facet of our lives. There are authority structures by which everything is governed, from the highest courts to the person who issues your dog's license. Besides national, regional, and local governments, there are authority structures for schools, businesses, churches, trade unions, garden clubs, sports teams, and even families. Even the most primitive Stone Age tribes have governmental structures with chiefs and village elders.

### Holes in the Walls

If "gates" refer to the choice of authority, then "walls" are a Bible symbol for the protection of authority in society. Satan sees the rightful structures in our society. He knows that if they are functioning properly, he cannot rule. The walls of authority shut him out. If the walls are broken down, he can and will rule. He can infiltrate. Where there is no authority or submission, he can infiltrate. Where there is no authority or submission to authority, where there is chaos and rebellion, Satan rules. The degree to which these institutions break down is the degree to which he governs. It is easy to understand why marriages, families, churches, and schools are under such vicious attack today.

The greatest manual for spiritual warfare is the Old Testament. The battles that were fought then in the earthly realm are exactly the same as those we now fight in the unseen world.

Satan incited and infiltrated armies of flesh and blood to destroy Israel. Today, he still seeks to destroy the people of God, and his strategies of battle have changed little.

In Old Testament Israel, people lived in cities. Their cities had high walls to keep the enemy out. If even a portion of the walls were broken down, the enemy soldiers were able to come in and plunder, and kill. When Nehemiah returned to the city of Jerusalem, before he built his own house, the house of God, or any other thing, he rebuilt the walls of the city. A city's walls were its greatest defense in a hostile world, and were always the first priority.

These ancient cities are a historical picture of what we now face in the unseen realm. Like the cities of the Old Testament, the governmental structures of society have walls. Though unseen, they are real walls of authority and protection. When these walls are torn down, the results are disastrous. In the unseen world, the devil is actively and effectively destroying the walls in three ways.

## Abdicating to the Devil

The first destroyer of these walls is _godless leadership_. When leaders do not live and lead according to biblical principles, and in agreement with the will of God, the walls of their authority crumble. Satan is allowed to rule through them. For instance, if a judge is corrupt and godless, he abdicates his leadership to unseen rulers. He does not realize he is handing over his court, but all under his authority will be open to Satan's attack. The same is true of all authority structures. Godless leadership breaks down the walls and allows rulers of the unseen world to rule. And they never miss an opportunity.

This is why I Timothy 2:1-2 directs us to pray for "all who are in authority." Every authority is under attack because the enemy wants to rule. We have a leadership crisis in much of society. We need to strengthen the walls of leadership. We need to intercede for our leaders. And as leaders ourselves, we need to be strong and lead with integrity. This will slow the enemy down. If on the other hand, we are constantly undermining authority, we are helping Satan's cause.

Another destroyer of society's protective walls is *neglect*—leaders who don't lead. Unfortunately, there are husbands who don't "husband," parents who don't parent, teachers who don't teach. To the extent that we neglect our responsibilities as leaders, we leave a vacuum for the rulers of darkness to rule in our place. For example, many fathers and mothers are too busy to spend time with their children, too busy to pass on moral values, or disciple and affirm them. This leaves their children vulnerable to the evil influences.

The third and most common destroyer of the walls is *rebellion.* Wherever I teach, I ask people to raise their hands if they have ever rebelled. Almost every hand in every group is raised. From little children to mature adults, we have all rebelled. Unfortunately, even in Christian circles rebellion is often excused. We say things like:

"Well, I'm just like that."

"I have a little stubborn streak in me."

"I'm not going to bc a 'yes' man."

"I like to have my own space."

"Sometimes you just have to stand up for your rights."

"I like to play the devil's advocate."

"It's just my personality."

We may defend our rebellious hearts with quaint little phrases, but we are wreaking tremendous damage to the walls of authority. The lines between compliance and resistance, support and opposition, and submission and defiance are too easily crossed when we give ourselves permission to be just "a little bit rebellious."

## What Rebellion Is and What It Is Not

First Samuel 15:23 reads "For rebellion is as the sin of divination, and insubordination is as iniquity and idolatry." This is a severe comparison. But we must realize that rebellion destroys the walls. Rebellion is a heart attitude that says, "I don't need rules. I don't need leaders or anyone telling me what to do."

Pure and simple, the spirit of rebellion is the rejection of authority. It is the desire for freedom from anything imposed upon us. The reason it is like witchcraft is because rebellion allows Satan to enter in. Rebellion and witchcraft accomplish the same thing in governmental structures and in individual lives: They both do business directly with the powers of darkness.

> *Let every person be in subjection to the governing authorities. For there is no authority except from God, and those which exist are established by God. Therefore he who resists authority has opposed the ordinance of God; and they who have opposed will receive condemnation upon themselves. For rulers are not a cause of fear for good behavior, but for evil. Do you want to have no fear of authority? Do what is good, and you will have praise from the same (Romans 13:1-3).*

Romans 13:1 does not say that every authority is godly. Not all are. We have corrupt policemen, judges, presidents, pastors, and parents. But the office of authority is established by God. It is His will that there be structures of authority, and that we all be in submission to those who hold positions of leadership. The leaders themselves may be evil, but the offices they hold exist as a wall of protection.

Authority in and of itself effectively hinders or slows down evil, according to Romans 13:3. It is a cause of fear for evildoers. A country that has a strong authority structure will limit evil, even though it is not Christian. A family that holds to family principles will slow down and hinder evil. The devil is held back by the walls of authority that surround these institutions. This is a universal principle of God. It affects everyone.

## Disobeying, But Not Rebelling

Does this mean we are to choose obedience to worldly authorities above obedience to God? No. In Acts 4, Peter was brought before the priests for preaching the Gospel. Their orders were in direct conflict with God's commands. Peter refused to obey them. He obeyed God rather than man, yet he did not attack the priests' authority. He didn't respond in rebellion. There can be a difference between rebellion and civil disobedience.

Submission to authority doesn't mean that we become "yes people" without opinions of our own. We can still stand against unrighteousness and falsehood. We can disagree, confront, and rebuke in the Spirit of Christ when we need to. But we must never tear down the structures or oppose leaders simply because they are in authority.

Satan is targeting families as families, trade unions as trade unions, and countries as countries. When we harbor rebellion, when we try to break down authority, we become his ally.

It is one thing to recognize Satan's attempts to break down walls. But what must we do about it? Ezekiel 22:30 says, "And I searched for a man among them who should build up the wall and stand in the gap...." God is looking for people who will rebuild walls through intercessory prayer. Now we know where the walls and the gaps are. They are all around us...the structures of society are crumbling. We are to fill these gaps as we intercede before God, and shut out the enemy on behalf of cities, families, schools, and individuals.

Ezekiel 13:4-5 is even more exacting in its challenge to take up our prophetic and intercessory responsibilities in society. "Your prophets have been like foxes among ruins. You have not gone up into the breaches, nor did you build the wall around the house of Israel to stand in the battle."

A fox makes himself a comfortable den in the ruins of a wall. This is often what Christians do while society disintegrates around them. We are called to rise up and repair the damage in the walls of society through warfare, prayer, and involvement.

## Principalities

The second function within demonic hierarchy is that of "principalities," often referred to as "territorial spirits." Principalities are not bigger, stronger, and more evil than other spirits in the kingdom of darkness. They don't necessarily have four more heads, or ten more eyes. Principalities are simply beings with broad areas of influence in Satan's kingdom.

To understand the word "principality," think of the word itself: A "prince" is a leader with title; the suffix "pality" has to do with both geography and demography. Geography is the study of land areas, and demography is the study of how people are grouped in society. The term principality reveals a most significant aspect of Satan's approach to our planet. Satan deploys his forces according to a map of the world. He hasn't haphazardly scattered his troops. They don't run around chaotically, bumping into one another.

The kingdom of darkness is as well-oiled as the best human military machine. Satan has particular battle plans for each geographic area and for each group of people. His plans for India differ from those for New York City. His strategies to rule over the homeless children of Colombia are distinct from those for the prostitutes of Amsterdam. Specific powers of darkness are assigned to specific areas and specific peoples.

Like any good general, Satan's plans to rule the earth have begun with good maps. He sees the world in segments. He sees empires, nations, regions, cities, precincts, and neighborhoods. He considers rural and urban population density. He is well acquainted with races, nationalities, tribes, clans, and even families. Satan is also a student of language groups, dialects, cultural heritage, and ethnic ancestry. He knows of every society, organization, and club. Satan knows his battleground. He knows his enemy, and is well prepared for the battle.

### Get Out Your Atlas

This is why we could stand with our toes in one country that is mostly Christian and have our heels in another that has no significant Christian witness. Many travelers have encountered this contrast from place to place. In one city we will observe the progress of God, and actually feel the positive, peaceful atmosphere. In another city we will experience the conflict, feel the oppression, and sense the domination of the powers of darkness. Even while crossing a bridge in the same city, some of us have experienced the change in the spiritual conditions. In Los Angeles, for instance, I have left one suburb for another and felt I had entered spiritually foreign territory. Then I saw it had more New Age shops, more cult centers, smaller and fewer churches, and a greater sense of an evil presence and overt occult activity.

This town, and many others, seems to draw like-minded people to it like a magnet.

God can give us a sensitivity to the spiritual influences at particular locations, but even without spiritual perception, we need only look at the statistics. Two cities can have highly different rates per capita of murder, violence, drug and alcohol addiction, prostitution, pornography, teenage pregnancies, abortions, adultery, divorces, and suicides. They can differ in the numbers of homosexuals or satanic and non-Christian cults and religions. They can experience differing rates of infant mortality, insanity, accidents, and diseases.

Satan deploys his forces and formulates his strategies according to the map. If we are serious about spiritual warfare, it is absolutely imperative that we become familiar with the geography and people groups of this planet. As Christians, we should be spending a great deal more time studying our atlases, the world, and those who live in it.

## Rattling His Cage

The devil shrugs off much of what we do. It isn't that we are doing wrong or carnal things, but that many of our efforts are of little consequence to Satan. However, when we pray according to a map, and when we begin to focus our prayers on the places and people groups Satan has marked for ownership and destruction, then we definitely capture his attention.

Is it a strange, new idea to pray for a country you've never been to? Does it seem odd to read about some tiny tribe in *National Geographic*, and then take that tribe earnestly before God in prayer? This only indicates how far off the track we are. In light of our Great Commission to "Go into all the world," *praying into all the world* should be our first response and our first commitment to win the world to Christ. Praying for people around the world is the responsibility of every Christian.

Praying geographically will shake up the devil and hinder his plans. But how can we pray for people when we don't know who they are or where they are? We can be sure Satan has done his research. We need to be learning and teaching geography in the Church. How can we pray for Sikkim if we think it's something we say to a dog? We should know that Sikkim is right beside Bhutan. Bhutan isn't that fashionable little shop in the mall, either. It is a country with only a handful of Christians. Few of us know where Mozambique is, but the devil has had a systematic plan for its destruction and bondage for centuries. Few Christians ever pray for Mauritania, which may be why there are so few Christians there. We don't know where it is or who lives there. But we can be sure the devil does.

The powers of darkness know about and have strategies for every group of people. The only thing standing in Satan's way is the Church. Spiritual warfare on a global scale means learning to pray geographically.

Daniel chapter 10 makes mention of the "prince of Persia," a principality over Persia. This principality has not died of old age, nor has he retired. He's probably still there, functioning in much the same way. The book of Daniel also mentions the princes of Greece. If there are princes of Persia and Greece, there are also princes of Scotland, Hawaii, London, Dallas, and even North Dallas.

Demography—the study of groupings of people—is an equally effective foundation upon which Satan formulates his strategies and assigns his forces. He has plans for every people group. He has a specific strategy and has assigned spirits for refugees, policemen, battered wives, telephone operators, the blind, businessmen, and every one of the countless tiny and separate groupings of humanity.

## A Football Game No One Would Pay to See

What is happening between the Church of Jesus Christ and the powers of darkness is much like a football game. In any football game, there are two teams with goal posts at opposite ends of the field. The object is for a team to get to the goal at the other end of the field, while preventing the opposing team from coming deep into its territory. The Church is lined up on the field with an elaborate formation of some size and complexity. We have senior pastors, junior pastors, youth pastors, pastors of old ladies, parking lot pastors, music directors, departments for this and that, elders, deacons, Sunday Schools,

Bible studies, and on and on. In countless business meetings, we have come up with all these wonderful goals and strategies.

These are good things. They are not bad or sinful or even carnal. Our team is standing on our side of the football field singing "The Church Triumphant."

On the other side of the field are the powers of darkness. If we think that they have anything other than an organized, thought through, systematic formation, we are greatly mistaken. Their formation consists of assignments to, and strategies for unwed mothers, orphans in Brazil, taxi drivers in New York, Laotians in California, Spanish-speaking people, the yacht club, and the tribe in the Amazon that no Christian has even heard of.

The only problem with this football game is that no one is getting his uniform dirty. At the kickoff, we stay on the sidelines practicing our formations while the devil makes touchdown after touchdown. No one would ever pay to see a sporting event in which there were two teams, but no competition.

I want to suggest a way to make this football game interesting. I suggest that the Church of Jesus Christ find out what the devil has been doing for the last few centuries, then move onto the field, and block him!

Spiritual warfare is not a football game, but we can still block the powers of darkness. We can engage the enemy and hinder his strategies for specific people by being specific in our prayers. Tackle the enemy according to his geographic and demographic strategies. For our offense, the Church should be praying geographically and making strategies for winning every area and all people groups to Christ. The enemy has been systematically wreaking havoc on the world. Entire countries are under bondage, almost void of Christian witness, because we the Church have not been specifically combating Satan. We have not known how Satan was doing his work in the world. We have been ignorant of his devices.

On the other hand, we have seen whole areas once resistant to the Gospel change dramatically as the direct result of Christians praying geographically and specifically. For example,

Nepal had only 29 Christians in 1959, and now there are 100,000.

## Whispering in Warfare

Another dramatic example of the results of specific prayer is Romania. Frank Barton (name changed for protection) began periodic visits as a non-resident missionary to Romania in 1983. The conditions horrified him. The secret police had murdered over 60,000 during Ceausescu's rule. Economic privation was so severe, each home could only have one dim light bulb on for a few hours each night. So many babies froze to death in the hospitals that the government passed a law saying that a baby is not a person until it is one month old—that way, those who died didn't show up on statistics.

As Frank went again and again to Romania, God led him to a small group of believers in a town called Timisoara. They met secretly in homes, and God began to speak to them about spiritual warfare. The Lord impressed them to come against the spirit of fear and the spirit of terror—these were controlling every aspect of Romanian society. They felt they were to go out in small groups late at night, taking prayer walks around their town. There, in front of various official buildings, Frank and the local Christians prayed against the principalities and powers—in whispers, lest the secret police hear them.

They felt foolish, but they kept obeying God. Over the months, things actually got worse. In February of 1989, two pastors disappeared—murdered by the secret police. Others were imprisoned, but the Christians continued to meet and do spiritual warfare. God spoke again, assuring them that victory was imminent.

Finally, on October 23, 1989, the word of the Lord came, telling them that a fire would begin in their town which would "blaze across Romania." What a difficult message to believe—especially for a little band of people, whispering their prayers in secret.

However, the spark began in Timisoara, just as God had said. It began with the house arrest on December 15, 1989, of a Reformed pastor named Laszlo Tokes. What usually followed such an arrest would be the disappearance of the minister, but this time was different. Word spread of Tokes' arrest, and instead of the usual cowed reaction, Christians streamed to the pastor's home, forming a human chain across the entrance. The police threatened them, but they began the first chant of the revolution: "Without fear, without fear! Liberty!"

The numbers grew. Some were taken away and tortured. But instead of the others scattering, more came—thousands more. Christians were joined by non-Christians, and no one seemed afraid. People walked up to the soldiers and bared their chests to the gun barrels, declaring, "We are winning! Down with Ceausescu!" News publications stated "hundreds perhaps thousands of unarmed men, women, and children were killed during December of 1989," but the crowds continued to grow. People walked up to the soldiers and knelt in prayer before them.

The flame had been lit. The army turned around and fought the secret police with the people, and the brutal reign of Ceausescu was over by Christmas of 1989. The newspapers of the country reported, "The band of fear and terror has been broken." Fear and terror—the same spirit powers God had directed a small group to pray against two years before.

This is just one story—many more were praying, not just for Romania, but for all of Eastern Europe. During the last thirty years, most of the Church has focused prayer for the suffering church in the communist world. What has happened there is proof that such focused praying against principalities and powers breaks their power. However, we still need to pray that God keeps this precarious openness in Eastern Europe.

## Powers

The third function in Satan's hierarchy is that of "powers" or "strongholds." This refers to kinds of evil and the demons assigned to those sins. It indicates a concentrated effort toward the building up of certain evils.

How does a defeated devil retain such a grip on the earth? When I was a young boy, I remember hearing a preacher proclaim that the devil was defeated. He said, "Jesus defeated the devil. We have the victory. He's out of business. He's absolutely unemployed." I walked out of the church thinking, "If the devil was defeated two thousand years ago, why is he still in our town?" It wasn't difficult for even a young boy to see how active this defeated devil was.

It's true that Satan was totally and eternally defeated. It is a fact worth celebrating that he has been vanquished. But it is equally true that this defeated devil is active in the earth today. How can this be? He is active in our society to the degree that people are sinning and living selfishly. He has precisely the amount of authority that we give him when we live in opposition to God. There is also a residue from those who have sinned throughout history. His freedom to move in our society is a gift to him by people like you and me who have sinned and continue to live selfishly.

Satan's activity is also determined by the nature of our sinning. The way in which we sin allows Satan to influence or coerce us in connection with those sins. He uses "power assignments," or demonic forces assigned according to the type of evil to which we give ourselves. So we have powers of greed, homosexuality, depression, fear, witchcraft, and so on. There can be as many powers as there are sins.

It's not as if the devil has a library of powers. He doesn't pull lust from the shelf and fling it at a city, causing everyone in that city to lust. That's not how it works. However, a city or even a country can collectively give itself over to lust or other sins. Because of the concentration of thousands of individual choices in that place, a power assignment of those particular sins is established. This is why one city can be characterized as a capital of pornography, while another city is known for its occult activities, while another is a center of gambling greed.

Power assignments also come into families when families give themselves over to particular sins. Even churches, although representatives of Christ, can have power assignments. A church that has a history of division and strife can have a power assignment of division and strife. Countries, cities, people groups, and even individuals can have power assignments. In some cases, the struggles of a people or place can be traced back hundreds of years to a time when people were giving themselves over to a specific practice of evil there.

In spiritual warfare, God can show us the nature of the powers in any particular situation. In homes, in cities, and in nations, God can and will give us an indication of entrenched powers. But we are never to simply know what these powers are and do nothing. We must take action. God will not merely satisfy our curiosity.

## Three Things We Should Do

**1. We should avoid the influence.**

If I find myself in a home full of strife, I must be careful not to be drawn into that contention. Similarly, this is why many well-meaning Christians blow it when they talk to Mormons or Jehovah's Witnesses. Christians start by sharing truth, but soon they are drawn into the contentious spirit. Contention will never win them to Christ because it is the same spirit under which these groups operate. We must share truth under the spirit of truth.

**2. We should pray specifically against spirit powers.**

God will show us the particular influencing spirit so that our prayers can be specific. We can then break these powers in the name of Jesus, and intercede for the Holy Spirit to come and heal the situation. The more specific we are in prayer, the more effective our prayers will be. For example, when we see a pattern of bondage in a family through generations, we simply need to recognize it and then in prayer, command it to be broken in the name of Jesus. If it is a power over a broader area, like a city or a nation, it will take more people praying in unity over a longer time to push it back.

**3. We should live in the opposite spirit.**

Living in the opposite spirit means that when we see greed prevailing in a situation, we become generous—subject, of course, to God's guidance in our giving. It also means that if we encounter depression, we decide to praise God and rejoice in all things. If we live in the opposite spirit, providing the opposite influence, we will break down these opposing powers. God is not calling us to act occasionally in response to powers, but to daily live whole, complete lives of spiritual warfare. By continually living in the opposite spirit before the powers of darkness and before people, we break through and change what's there.

I regularly take evangelism teams into different parts of the world, and in each place we seek God as to the predominant powers at work. One country has the highest suicide rate in the world. Missionaries have gone home from there depressed and defeated in record numbers. It doesn't take any special perception to see that powers of depression have made their home there. During one short-term missions outreach to this country, after being there only two weeks, individuals came to me saying:

"I'm so depressed."

"We're not accomplishing anything here."

"I'm useless."

If we don't recognize specific powers in a place, we can become susceptible to their influence.

One other thing we should realize about Satan's hierarchy—his rulers, principalities, and powers: The division of these functions is not hard and fast. We could compare it to a human corporation with several vice presidents, each one carrying various portfolios of responsibility. It is the same with rulers, principalities, and powers. Sometimes a principality can also be a ruler, exerting control over a human authority structure. A power could also be a principality, as in the case of those ruling over Romania. The same demon can have various functions.

Many activities of the enemy are functions that intersect in the heavenlies. If we ask the Holy Spirit, He will reveal how Satan is working in any given place or situation. We can then come against his works in specific prayer. The Lord may lead us to pray against a principality over a country, or against a spirit attacking families, or against a demon keeping people in atheism. As we do, we will be thwarting Satan's plans on earth.

Simple obedience in prayer is far more important than attempts to make elaborate categories of the spirit world.

## Prong #2: Forces of Darkness

Another way Satan assaults humanity is through forces of darkness. "Forces of this darkness" (Eph. 6:12) is a Bible term to show the workings of Satan's kingdom. The forces of darkness do two things: They lie, and they hinder the truth.

## Lying Spirits

We need to understand that a bastion of demonic spirits has been sent onto this planet expressly to keep men's minds in darkness. These beings deceive us about everything from simple little lies, to big, complicated lies like Hinduism, Islam, and Buddhism. For example, one lying spirit is the angel Moroni. This demon, headquartered in Salt Lake City, is blinding the eyes of millions of people throughout the earth. We know this lying spirit's name because of his appearance to Joseph Smith. But I believe there are other demons whom we don't know, who are assigned to every major religion and cult on earth. "...The god of this world has blinded the minds of the unbelieving, that they might not see the light of the gospel of the glory of Christ, who is the image of God" (II Cor. 4:4).

Many of us have believed things in the past that we no longer believe. We were in a measure of darkness. Our whole lives are a process of gaining further light—of seeing falsehoods exposed, and embracing the truth of God's Word. The enemy's job is to continually hinder this process, hiding the light and blinding us with falsehood. A constant barrage of lies is aimed at every person's mind. These spirits lie to us about God—that He does not exist, or that He is not good and loving. They give us wrong concepts about others. Or they tell us lies about ourselves, making us hate ourselves. This is all darkness.

### Enormous Conspiracies of Lies

As I've already mentioned, sometimes the enemy's lies are a complex network of ideas. False religions and deceptive philosophies are no small activity on the earth. The depth and sophistication of these beliefs, and the many tributaries from which they merge into one stream, are evidence of the enormous conspiracy to deceive the minds of men. The effectiveness of these lies is seen in entire nations and in huge people groups. In I Timothy 4:1, Paul predicted the rise of these "deceitful spirits and doctrines of demons."

Every cult and non-Christian religion in the world springs from Satan's complex network of deception. This system has been conceived in the pits of hell, carefully crafted to enslave minds. Recently, we have been inundated by Western-looking, but very Eastern thoughts. Called the New Age movement, it is nothing more than the "old age" lie told to Eve in the garden:

> *You can be a god and establish your own reality, your own truth, and your own morality. You don't have to die—you can reincarnate. God is not a person, but a force that is in everyone and everything. You can discover this all-pervasive God-energy as you yield yourself to a higher consciousness and deeper self.*

This supposed *new* enlightenment is really *old* darkness, and has been at the core of every false religion and cult throughout history. Now we can see its message in current music, popular TV programs, movies, trends, and seminars. It has captured Hollywood celebrities, Pentagon officials, and has even reached into local elementary schools. We Christians must be able to detect this lie and combat its influence.

### Not Political, Nor Scientific

Other systems may not seem to be related, but they are. It is difficult to criticize communism or evolution without being immediately labeled as a right-wing fundamentalist. But communism and evolution are covered with thin veneers of politics and science. Ignoring the political and the scientific trappings, we need to see them through spiritual warfare eyes. Communism, more than any other system, has fervently attempted to hinder the Gospel, crush the Church, and rid people of hope in God. When any philosophy or ideology opposes God, it is no longer primarily political, but spiritual.

Evolution's scientific credentials are also of no significance from a spiritual warfare point of view. Rather than arguing over strata and fossils, we only need to look at the results of evolutionary theory in the hearts and minds of men. Evolution has been the cesspool from which communism, humanism, existentialism, and even Nazism have emerged. It is an anti-God philosophy, justified with ludicrous propositions, and cleverly disguised as science. No other philosophy vomited onto this planet has damned more souls than evolution. No competitor from the pits of hell has half of its artful deceit.

Religions, philosophies, and ideologies must become spiritual warfare issues for Christians. As spiritual warriors, we can deal with them by praying, and standing against them in the spiritual realm. And we can deal with them by continually standing up for the truth. Our stand must be against every form of falsehood. If Christians are anything, they are the guardians and proclaimers of truth.

## Hindering the Truth

These forces are not just interested in spreading lies, but also in hindering truth. It may not often occur to us, but there are demonic forces assigned to hindering the preaching of the Gospel. They can be called spiritual anti-evangelists, who do everything in their power to keep Christians from sharing, and people from hearing the Gospel.

Many of us casually approach evangelism as something we do if we get the chance. Some will be receptive and some won't. At times we don't feel like doing it, and sometimes we do. We know it is our responsibility to share the Gospel, but we are not overly enthusiastic. Have you ever wondered why this is? Why does it feels so awkward? And why aren't more people receptive when we finally get around to doing it? Could it be that there are forces of darkness hampering our attitudes and efforts in evangelism? There is a demonic system trying to talk us out of evangelism. These beings say, "Don't be a Bible-banger. You're not an evangelist. You look ridiculous. People will just reject you. What makes you think you're right and they're wrong? Don't do it."

## Two Things Demons Hate

Other than effective intercession, there are two things that the powers of darkness absolutely hate in the lives of believers: humility and effective evangelism. Humility tears up the roots of pride and deception in the lives of those whom Satan rules. Satan was defeated by Christ's humility at the Cross. The powers of darkness also hate evangelism because it invades their territory.

We can have all kinds of meetings, sing-alongs, and "bless-me clubs." The devil couldn't care less. But if we move into his territory and start to free souls from his grasp, we must be prepared for all-out warfare. He will lie to us about our abilities. He will influence us toward fear. He will hold back our finances so that we can't go to the mission field. He will stop at nothing to keep us from spreading the Gospel. We must not just take opportunities when they fall into our laps. We must go on the offensive. We must be determined to share the Gospel.

According to Luke 10:2, "The harvest is plentiful, but the laborers are few; therefore beseech the Lord of the harvest to send out laborers into His harvest." We should never assume that Gospel preaching is enough. Neither is it enough to just get more people doing it. No matter how many Christians respond to God's call to "go into all the world," the laborers will still be few in light of the forces of darkness trying to hinder it. The laborers will be "few" as long as there is even one soul to save.

Should this discourage us? No. But we must learn this: We cannot separate spiritual warfare from world evangelism. What can we do? Just pray and rebuke the devil? If we are in a dark room, we do not simply rebuke the darkness. We turn on the light. If we want to rid the world of darkness, we must do everything in our power to turn on the light of Jesus Christ. We should sing it, preach it, write it, dramatize it, do whatever it takes to proclaim the Gospel. We should never be against any method if it proclaims the truth. And all the while, we must be engaging in spiritual warfare along with our evangelism.

"Therefore, my beloved brethren, be steadfast, immovable, always abounding in the work of the Lord, knowing that your toil is not in vain in the Lord" (I Cor. 15:58).

# Prong #3: Attack on the Individual

The third prong of the assault by the kingdom of darkness is that of wicked spirits. Wicked spirits are not interested in geographic areas, nor in communism, but in the individual. Wicked spirits influence individual behavior. We have already dealt fully in Chapter Four with the way these forces attack the individual—especially through the mind, the heart, and the mouth. Tempting spirits promote sin, and if successful, draw people into bondage.

The concern of these spirits is not a group, but an *individual*. We have talked earlier about guardian angels. It is possible that a demon has also been assigned to each of us. This shouldn't alarm us, because we are kept by the power of God if we are Christians. Nevertheless, Satan is interested in the individual.

Wicked spirits try to influence our behavior. We are being tempted to do evil constantly by the enemy's pressure on our thoughts, attitudes, appetites, and wills. But notice, it is an influence, not a cause. Flip Wilson had a popular routine during the Sixties called..."The Devil Made Me Do It!" This may be good comedy, but it's not the way it works. People claim to be helpless, but they are not. For instance, even a kleptomaniac will not steal when he knows he's being watched.

### Descent into Bondage

There is a progression, however. Everything wrong starts with an **influence**. We're tempted...we feel like doing it. We can ask for God's grace and refuse it, or we can acquiesce. If we give in to the influence, we get a **"weight on our will."** It will be easier to do that particular sin a second time. With each repetition, the sin becomes easier as we begin to **dull our conscience**. We can get to the place where a sin doesn't even seem wrong. This is how a hit man can shoot someone, then go and enjoy a good meal. It doesn't bother him anymore.

If we continue in evil, we develop **"habits of sin."** Habits can be very strong. Two common mistakes happen at this point. First, we become convinced that it is our basic human nature and cannot be cured. Secondly, we think we are possessed. This isn't true—we aren't possessed yet. It is just a habit, deeply ingrained, like many other things we do without thinking. For example, when I go to New Zealand, driving is all backward. When I slide behind the wheel of the car, the steering wheel is on the right side instead of the left. I pull away from the curb to the right and have to concentrate on staying in the left lane. I can't just drive on the right side, get pulled over by a policeman and then explain...

"I can't help myself! You don't know my background. Driving on the right side has been in my family for generations. I've lived in an atmosphere of driving on the right all my life. I'm only human—I have weaknesses. I can't change immediately! Can't I drive in the middle for awhile, just until I get used to it?"

No, I can't do that. The first time I drove on the left side of the road, I did it immediately and successfully—there was no "demon of right lane driving" from which I had to be delivered. I simply broke the habit of years. Habit patterns can be deep, but they can be broken with God's grace and with our commitment.

However, if we continue in a habit of sin, we can develop a **bondage.** A bondage means that there is a supernatural element to our problem. The enemy now has a grip on a function of our personality. Traditionally, we have talked of a progression, with people being obsessed, oppressed, or possessed. But I have stopped using these words because it is hard to define where one stops and another begins. The word "possessed" doesn't appear in original Scriptures; the word used is simply "demonized." This is what I am calling a bondage.

It is possible to have a bondage that does not consume your entire personality and function—you are merely bound in a certain part of your personality. Whatever the bondage, and whatever the degree, if you are bound, you need to be set free in Jesus' name.

Spiritual warfare deals with two levels: the big, or cosmic level, and the individual, personal level. In dealing with the kingdom of darkness, we stand against the rulers, principalities, and powers in nations, in people groups, and in authority structures. And we must bring freedom from bondage to individuals through prayer, intercession, and personal ministry. We stand against evil influences in their lives, and in ours as well. We must be resolute in our efforts to share the Gospel and bring light wherever there is darkness. It is not too great a task, if we go on to learn how strong we can be in the Lord. We can become men and women with God-given authority, winning victories on every level.

# CHAPTER EIGHT

# Using Your God-given Authority

It is possible to become discouraged by the size and sophistication of Satan's forces. However, God has established an even stronger army. It is us...every Christian; it is *you*. Maybe this leaves you even more disheartened! But there is hope. If we are not confident in God's army of Christians, if we are unsure of ourselves, it is because we do not yet know who we are, or in whose authority we operate.

If I were to ask you if Christians had authority over the powers of darkness, you would probably say, "Amen, Brother!" But what would happen if you were suddenly confronted by a demonized person? You might call your pastor for help, and he might in turn call another pastor! We are not convinced we have authority. We know it mentally, we're the first to say we do. But we cannot walk in spiritual authority because deep down, we doubt it. Why? Because we have mistakenly confused our authority with our emotions.

## What Authority is Not

There are some days when we come out of church brimming with confidence. The teaching was great, the worship was wonderful, and we're ready to take on the devil. Two days later, we're wondering if we are saved. We confuse our authority with our feelings.

Some think of authority as a personality type. We speak of someone as a "man of authority." What we are really saying is, the man has the kind of personality we associate with authority. Perhaps he's tall, has a deep voice, knits his brow, clenches his fist, and talks firmly. Shy and retiring types say, "Well, I'm not the authoritative type." But the basis of our authority is not personality or feelings. It is not the product of our maturity, or of how long we have been Christians. Every Christian needs to know the basis of his or her spiritual authority.

The enemy will do everything he can to keep us from becoming convinced of our authority. If he can make us think authority is a feeling, he can keep us from acting when we don't *feel* confident. We are no threat to Satan if we are uncertain. We will constantly waver unless we rely on the fact that we have authority. Perhaps Satan's greatest fear is that we will come into the assurance of our authority and walk in that assurance.

In this chapter we will see that the basis for our spiritual authority is a legal one. It is a legal reality that does not waver because of our unbelief, and is as real as any transaction. In fact, it's a legal arrangement much like marriage. When I ask people if they are married I never hear, "Well, I'm not sure. Sometimes I feel married, and sometimes I just don't know." They will always say, "Yes" or "No." If we are married, we are totally convinced of it at all times, and have a legal document to prove it. Feelings, thoughts, and personalities do not change the reality of that legal arrangement.

Our spiritual authority is just as real and legal as marriage. It is not just a concept; it's an actual thing.

### How We Lost It

In order to understand how authority works, we must go back to the beginning. When God made mankind in the Garden of Eden, He created him different from the animals. He gave man free will, as well as dominion or authority. All authority was in God's hands, but in the Garden a limited portion of that authority changed hands. God delegated some of His authority to man and He has never taken it back. This is why people are now doing all kinds of evil and God is not stopping them.

Some feel this transfer of authority has diminished God's authority or sovereignty. It has not. God had, God has, and God always will have all authority. He has total jurisdiction over everything. He is all-powerful, and rules without limit or question. God is able, however, to delegate portions of His authority.

Presidents of large corporations hire people and give them jobs as directors, managers, and supervisors. With each position comes a set of responsibilities and the authority to fulfill them. The authority is a portion of the president's. It is still under his control, but is delegated to various employees. Similarly, God has delegated authority to man, but still reigns over man.

Satan in the form of a serpent was in the Garden when God gave authority to man. Later the devil approached Eve. Why? Why did he go to such lengths to deceive her? He did so partly to get back at God—to hurt Him. But there was more. Adam and Eve had something of tremendous value to Satan. Satan wanted the authority God had given to man. Although he was on the planet, the devil did not have authority and jurisdiction over the planet. Satan realized that authority is a legally based reality, so he went to Eve and tempted her. What he was really saying was, "Why don't you sign over some of your authority to me?"

Satan knew that man could use or misuse the authority given to him. When man disobeyed God, Satan was able to usurp man's authority. Just as God transferred some of His authority to man, so man passed it on to Satan.

Yet Satan does not have complete authority. He cannot simply rule the world. He operates the same way today as he did in Eden, usurping what God has given man. Man gave his authority to Satan, but Satan can only use it through man. He can only *influence* the world to the degree that man chooses to sin and live in disobedience to God. This is what we might call the balance of power.

After man sinned in the Garden, God rebuked all parties involved and said, "And I [God] will put enmity between you [Satan] and the woman, and between your seed and her seed; he shall bruise you on the head, and you shall bruise him on the heel" (Gen. 3:15).

God promised to bruise Satan's head—not directly, but through the seed of the woman. The seed of Satan would in turn bruise mankind's heel. This established the grounds for spiritual warfare. Satan is working through mankind to do his business on the planet. And God is working through mankind to defeat the enemy. This is what has been happening throughout history.

## The Attack on Children

"Enmity" means a barrier of contention or strife. The "seed of Satan" is that which Satan spawns. Since he cannot have children, his seed is that which he is able to bring forth in men. The seed of the woman is three things: It is, first of all, all who are born from Eve—the human race. Satan's attack on the seed of the woman is seen primarily in his attack on all human children.

It is easy to see throughout history and today that Satan zealously targets children, seeking their bondage and destruction. The enmity between children and the enemy is especially strong. Children are new and innocent, the "seed of woman." From the fires of Molech in Old Testament times, where parents sacrificed newborn babies on the red-hot arms of idols; to present-day war atrocities, abortion, drug addiction, and child pornography; children are under direct attack from Satan.

Secondly and thirdly, the "seed of the woman" refers to the children of Israel, and to the Lord Jesus Christ.

God proclaimed that the seed of Satan will bruise man's heel. If a man has a bruised heel, he will not be able to go as far or as fast as he might. The results of sin have bruised the heel of every man. Our hair falls out or becomes gray. We get wrinkles and lose our eyesight. Our strength wanes and our minds slow down. From the moment we are born, we head for the grave. Romans 5:12 says, "...Through one man sin entered into the world, and death through sin, and so death spread to all men...." This is our bruised heel.

## Why Is the Old Testament So Violent?

God also promised Satan that the seed of the woman would bruise his head. I think Satan was quite concerned with this promise of judgment. He began to keep his eyes open, looking for the seed. Sure enough, Eve brought forth "seed." She gave birth to two boys: Cain and Abel. As they grew, Satan was able to influence Cain, but saw that Abel was much like he knew God to be. Remembering that the seed would bruise his head, and perceiving a threat from the seed, perhaps Satan provoked Cain to slay Abel. But even that didn't stop God's plan. Eve gave birth to Seth, and eventually through Seth came the nation of Israel and ultimately, Jesus.

The story of Cain and Abel is really the story of the whole of history. In fact, from a spiritual warfare perspective, the Old Testament can be summed up in two statements:

- It is the historical record of God bearing the seed of the woman through the nation of Israel to bring Jesus Christ into the world.

- It is the history of Satan's attempts to corrupt and destroy the seed that would bruise his head.

This is why there was so much fighting and violence in the Old Testament. From Adam and Eve, through Noah, Abraham, David, and Mary, God brought the seed of the woman onward, while Satan did all he could to destroy it.

So many Christians puzzle at the violence and the brutality of the Old Testament. Some even avoid it for fear it will cause them to doubt the lovingkindness of God, as shown through the New Testament. But we need to see that the battles of the Old Testament were for the preservation of the seed of the woman that would result in Jesus Christ.

## A Battle For the Human Race

Throughout the Old Testament, Satan tried desperately to either destroy or corrupt the seed of the woman, which he knew was in the children of Israel. It seemed everybody was fighting Israel. Why would people like the Amalekites attempt to destroy Israel unless demonic forces incited them, hoping to destroy the seed of the woman? The battle to preserve the seed was a flesh and blood battle. Blood flowed and little mercy was shown for those who threatened the seed.

Those battles were physical and took place in the earthly realm, and yet Israel was also in the midst of spiritual warfare. The battle was *physical* because the seed of the woman was a *physical seed* that would bring a *physical manifestation* of God into the earth *to die physically* on a cross. In order for Satan to destroy the seed, it would take a physical victory. It was a battle which would determine whether or not the Messiah would come into the world. It was a battle for the salvation of the human race.

### Why Did Babies Have to Be Killed?

Why did God have little babies killed? And why did He have Israel destroy one tribe and leave the next alone? Did God just have bad days—was He cruel one day and kind the next? Was He so angry and vengeful that He lost His composure? In answer, we have a number of choices: We can question the character of God, thinking Him to be cruel; we can ignore these things, refusing to ask questions and denying that we have doubts; or lastly, we can trust God's character, knowing that if He ordered entire tribes killed, He had good reasons.

Because God is righteous in all His ways, and kind in all His deeds, (Ps. 145:17) we know that even when He brought judgment, He had good purposes—life purposes.

The struggles in the Old Testament often had sexual implications. A large part of the heathen religions was sexual. For instance, sodomy, lesbianism, and bisexuality were not only encouraged, but commanded in rituals of worship to Ashere and Baal. [2] Satan, knowing the weaknesses of men, enticed them to worship idols—worship that almost always included sexual activity. Using sexual enticement and perversion, Satan sought to corrupt the seed before it could bruise his head.

It is possible that this sexual activity also brought about a tremendous amount of venereal disease, which produced retar-

---

2 Pratney, Winkie, *Devil Take the Youngest*, Shreveport, Huntington House 1985

dation, deformation, and even death. Unchecked, venereal diseases could wipe out an entire city. Could this have been why on occasion God ordered the total destruction of Israel's enemies? At times God commanded that every man, woman, and child, and even the livestock, be put to death.

## A Radical Act of Mercy

God has always been kind and just. He wasn't mean in the Old Testament and kind in the New. He has never changed. I believe that on occasion, Israel was confronted by tribes riddled with disease. These tribes lived in total disobedience to God, worshiped the vilest of gods, and were being used of the devil to destroy Israel, perhaps even the entire human race. The only way to rid humanity of the threat and to protect the seed from corruption was for God to remove these tribes from the face of the earth. It was a radical act of mercy and love for the whole of mankind.

Although Satan's attempts to destroy and corrupt the seed did not work, there were a number of times in Israel's history where they succumbed. They often sinned, following after false gods, but there were always some who remained true, preserving the seed. Eventually, when the time was absolutely right, God fulfilled His promise. Galatians 4:4 says, "But when the fulness of the time came, God sent forth His Son, born of a woman" (the seed of the woman).

When Satan failed to destroy the seed of the woman before the Messiah's birth, he redoubled his efforts to destroy the Christ child. He incited Herod to kill all the baby boys in Bethlehem under two years old (see Matthew 2). Thousands of infants were slaughtered—all in the attempt to destroy the seed. Joseph and Mary were forced to flee to Egypt to keep baby Jesus from certain death.

Jesus grew up in Nazareth, but we have little information about those years. We can be sure, however, that Satan sought His destruction, both physically and morally. The Bible does tell us in Hebrews 4:15 that Jesus was "tempted in all things as we are, yet without sin." It would seem that Satan continued his efforts to corrupt the seed. Jesus really was tempted. He didn't just go through the motions. As He grew up and entered adulthood, He was confronted with everything that is common to man. There is no temptation we have experienced that Jesus did not also experience. And yet, Jesus prevailed without sin.

The Bible tells us that Jesus went to be baptized by His cousin John in the waters of the Jordan River. When He was baptized, the Holy Spirit in the form of a dove came upon Him and a voice from heaven said, "This is My beloved Son, in whom I am well pleased." After thousands of years of battle, God proclaimed to the world that here stood the Son of God, the seed of the woman.

## The Devil's Feverish Attempts

Jesus went from the Jordan River into the wilderness to be tempted. For the first time in human form, and truly as the promised seed, Jesus stood before Lucifer, the fallen archangel, and probably a multitude of other demonic powers. What followed was not a ceremony, but a pitched, fevered battle. Satan exerted all the influence he could muster to corrupt the seed that would bruise his head.

Jesus submitted Himself to temptation. After fasting for 40 days, He was tempted to turn stones into bread. It was a temptation to use His spiritual power to feed Himself. Unfortunately, many try to use the miracle-working power of God for selfish purposes. But Jesus said no.

The second temptation was for Jesus to jump from a high place, knowing that God would stop His fall and protect Him. It would be a publicity stunt that would bring Him the attention of the world. Jesus' importance would be evidenced by the fact that He could even move the hand of God to protect Him. The crowds would come and Jesus would have His following that very day. It was an appeal to pride.

Some of us often do things to get attention. We'll promote ourselves to people, highlight our gifts and talents, and make lots of noise just to get a following. We often raise ourselves above the purposes of God and set out to prove our self-importance to the world. But Jesus said no to this. He would serve humanity by laying His life down, not by manipulation for the attention of man.

The third temptation was to gain authority. Satan offered Jesus the very authority he had stolen from men, if Jesus would worship him. Some contend that Satan was telling Jesus a lie. But it was true. It had to be true in order to be a temptation. As long as man lived in sin and selfishness, the authority was Satan's.

Satan's offer was a temptation for power, prominence, control, and governmental authority—without the suffering and shame of the Cross. Jesus said no. He was going to defeat the enemy, not through power, but through humility. The desire for power never accomplishes the purposes of God. The Church does not need power without humility. The Church should only use the power of God in the humility of Christ.

Throughout the three years of Jesus' ministry, the Bible records many attempts to kill Him. He escaped until His ministry was complete. At the right time, Jesus willingly handed Himself over to evil men to do with Him whatever their evil minds could devise. Jesus said in John 10:18 concerning His life, "No one has taken it away from Me, but I lay it down on My own initiative."

## Why Did Jesus Have to Suffer, Too?

Whatever could enter into the minds of men—the most evil, depraved, obscene, torturous crimes that hell could inspire—all such acts must have been done to Jesus. We have no idea of the pain and humiliation He suffered. In discussing the sufferings and death of Jesus, the Bible uses generalities: He was "despised," "rejected," "unjustly treated and accused," and "mocked and scourged." Why did God allow Jesus to go through these unspeakable sufferings before His death? Could it be that Jesus not only died for our sins, but as stated in the description of Jesus' atoning work, "The punishment that brought us peace was upon him" (Isaiah 53:5 NIV)? Jesus became an object of hate and rejection, suffering outrageous injustice, that we might have peace when we suffer the same. Just as we have by faith received forgiveness and cleansing from sin, so we need to believe that God will give us peace during our times of grief, humiliation, and betrayal.

Jesus suffered for us. Finally, He was nailed to a cross and, slowly and painfully, He died for our sins.

The Bible tells us that upon Jesus' death, He went to Hades. Opinions vary about Hades, but it seems evident that it consists of two sections. One section, called Paradise, is the place Jesus referred to when He told the thief on the cross beside Him, "Today you shall be with Me in Paradise" (Luke 23:43). It is the place where the spirits of the righteous await the Resurrection. The other part of Hades is the place where the spirits of the wicked wait. While in Hades, Jesus paid a visit to both sides. While in Paradise, He preached to the captives. These spirits were captive because Satan held the keys to sin and death, but they were not in torment. Ephesians 4:8 says, "When He ascended on high, He led captive a host of captives."

## The Legal Basis For Our Authority

Jesus also went to the other side of Hades, the domain of Satan. While there He established the legal basis for our authority. He stripped Satan of the authority he had stolen from man. Colossians 2:15 reads, "When he had disarmed the rulers and authorities, He made a public display of them, having triumphed over them through Him." Jesus now has the keys to death and Hades, and Satan is no longer legally in control. Revelation 1:18 says, "I was dead, and behold, I am alive forevermore, and I have the keys of death and of Hades." Jesus took from the devil the legal right to the balance of power on this planet.

This is why God had to become a man. He came primarily to atone for sin. Authority had been given to man in and through his free will. Man had then used that free will to give away his authority. Therefore, God had to either cancel man, cancel free will, or become a man Himself. He chose to become a man so that He could say no to temptation for 30 years as a man, reject the enemy in the wilderness as a man, and choose to lay His life down and give up His spirit as a man. He was willing to humble Himself to the point of death as a man so that as a man, He could qualify to take back what the first man chose to give away.

Jesus also established our authority, destroying the devil's works. First John 3:8 says, "The Son of God appeared for this purpose, that He might destroy the works of the devil." The works of the devil are the "bruised heel of man," or the results of sin in the human situation. Disease, suffering, depression, ignorance, fear, broken hearts, wounded spirits, war, famine, and hatred—the sum of what Satan has been able to achieve in and through men. Jesus destroyed these works.

This is why Jesus spotlighted the portion of Isaiah concerning Himself: "The Spirit of the Lord is upon Me, because He anointed Me to preach the gospel to the poor [those in need]. He has sent Me to proclaim release to the captives, and recovery of sight to the blind, to set free those who are downtrodden, to proclaim the favorable year of the Lord" (Luke 4:18-19). According to Acts 10:38, "You know of Jesus of Nazareth, how God anointed Him with the Holy Spirit and with power, and how He went about doing good, and healing all who were oppressed by the devil; for God was with Him." Jesus healed, helped, delivered, and ministered to everyone He met who was oppressed by the powers of darkness.

By destroying the works of the devil on the Cross, He also enabled us to do the same—to reach out to the oppressed, the downtrodden, and the brokenhearted. Before ascending back to heaven, He gave us a mandate to reverse the works of the devil. Included in the Great Commission were the statements: "In My name they will cast out demons...they will lay hands on the sick, and they will recover" (Mark 16:17-18). This is our stewardship of the authority Jesus retrieved on our behalf.

### We've Changed Neighborhoods

Our authority is not only based on what Jesus did to the devil, but on what He did for us. Colossians 1:13-14 tells us that God "delivered us from the domain of darkness, and transferred us to the kingdom of His beloved Son, in whom we have redemption, the forgiveness of sins."

We need to recognize that no one has ever come to Christ without first of all being a child of the devil, living in the kingdom of darkness. We have all been there. Being a Christian is not just thinking new thoughts or acting new ways. It is not a product of our heritage. Christ didn't simply make good men better. Every Christian has packed his bags and taken up residence in a new place. We have been delivered from sin, selfishness, death, darkness, destruction, and ourselves. We have been delivered from a dominion of darkness and transplanted into the Kingdom of Jesus Christ. Every day of our lives we should remind ourselves of our old neighborhood and thankfully remember who it was who delivered us.

We are presently in either one of two places. There is no middle ground. We are either in the kingdom of darkness or in the Kingdom of God's Son. Christians who have repented, who believe in Christ's atonement, are definitely in the Kingdom of God's Son. We need to reassure ourselves that our new home is in the kingdom of light, and never doubt it. Often subsequent work needs to take place in our lives. But the effectiveness of Christ's further work in us is based on our confidence that we have indeed been transferred.

Not only did Jesus deliver us, but He gives us power to live the life He called us to live. We can consistently live through anything we might face by the power of God dwelling within us. First John 4:4 says, "Greater is He who is in you than he who is in the world." Many Christians have never lived a minute of victory or peace since their salvation. They simply do not know that the same power that brought them out of sin can keep them through Mondays and Tuesdays. How are we going to take on principalities over nations if we can't be victorious through Tuesday?

Do we really know that greater is He who lives in us than he who is in the world? I'm not sure many of us really believe this wonderful truth. I hear Christians grumble and complain about their situations. They believe they are victims of leadership, victims of unfair rules, victims of the church they attend, victims of their husbands, or victims of their children. But what they are really saying is, "Greater is he who is in the world and in all my circumstances than He who is in me!"

Christians are quite impressed with the works of the enemy in the world. One man told me, "I recently went to New York. You wouldn't believe the oppression there! I could feel the enemy all around me. I just had to get out of there." I've heard Christians argue about which place, country, or city was the darkest and most oppressive. Why are we so impressed with the oppression when there is something greater in us?

## Jesus In Us Won't Shrivel Before Satan

We seem to think that Christians have a low threshold of tolerance to oppression. We are convinced that if a young Christian attends a secular college, he won't survive. It's true. He won't survive unless he truly believes that within every Christian is a power far greater than anything the world and the enemy can muster.

Do we really believe that Jesus and any one Christian are stronger than any force in the universe? Is there any place I can go where the forces around me are stronger than Jesus in me? What good is having Christ in me and His authority at my disposal if I can't handle my job, live in New York, witness in the red-light district of Amsterdam, walk in the slums of Bangkok, or sit in the home of a Hindu? Jesus in us does not shrivel up when confronted by oppression. There is no place, no circumstance, and no pressure in which Christians are not greater. This secular, humanistic, and even satanic society is *less* than that which is in every Christian.

Satan knows that if we can be kept from confidently believing in the authority God gives us, then we will be out of the race, sidelined by our doubts, fears, and weaknesses. We must know that the Spirit of the living God dwells in us. It is a reality that Satan's lies cannot change. But if we don't embrace the truth— that greater is He who is in me—then it might as well not be true. We will agree with Satan's lie, victims of our circumstances and the powers of darkness. Greater is He who is in us. This is either true or false. We must believe it. We must speak it out to the enemy. We must agree with God and with the truth. And we must live the life He has called us to live, knowing that He can and will maintain us.

*Who shall separate us from the love of Christ? Shall
tribulation, or distress, or persecution, or famine, or
nakedness, or peril, or sword? Just as it is written, "For
Thy sake we are being put to death all day long; we
were considered as sheep to be slaughtered." But in all
these things we overwhelmingly conquer through Him
who loved us. For I am convinced that neither death,
nor life, nor angels, nor principalities, nor things present, nor things to come, nor powers, nor height, nor
depth, nor any other created thing, shall be able to
separate us from the love of God, which is in Christ
Jesus our Lord (Romans 8:35-39).*

## Jesus Handed Back What We Had Given Away

Jesus also gave us authority to exercise. Luke 10:19 reads,

*Behold, I have given you authority to tread upon serpents
and scorpions, and over **all** the power of the enemy, and nothing
shall injure you (emphasis added).* As individuals we have
authority over all the combined powers of the enemy. This is an
incredible, wondrous truth. Everything at Satan's disposal—
every demon, every coven, every cult and religion, every work,
and every influence—is subject to the authority given to us by
Jesus.

When Jesus rose from the dead after ripping the usurped
authority from Satan's hands, He did not immediately go to
heaven. He stopped off to see the eleven remaining disciples.
These very human, very weak men had fled, frightened out of
their minds. Peter had denied even knowing Him. Unbelievably,
Jesus sought out these men. Jesus did not rebuke them. He didn't
say, "I told you so" to Peter. He affirmed them and did something quite amazing. He breathed on them, saying, "Receive the
Holy Spirit. If you forgive the sins of any, their sins have been
forgiven them; if you retain the sins of any, they have been
retained" (John 20:22-23). Jesus handed to them the authority
He had taken from Satan. The authority legally changed hands
once more and belonged to man again.

*I pray that the eyes of your heart may be enlight-
ened, so that you may know what is the hope of His*

*calling, what are the riches of the glory of His inheri-
tance in the saints, and what is the surpassing greatness
of His power toward us who believe. These are in
accordance with the working of the strength of His
might which He brought about in Christ, when He
raised Him from the dead, and seated Him at His right
hand in the heavenly places, far above all rule and
authority and power and dominion, and every name
that is named, not only in this age, but also in the one
to come. And He put all things in subjection under His
feet, and gave Him as head over all things to the church,
which is His body, the fulness of Him who fills all in all
(Ephesians 1:18-23).*

## Now It's Up to Us

Man again has authority, based on what Christ did on the
Cross and through His resurrection. Man can still employ Satan
through selfishness and sin, but the balance of power on the
earth rests with man in the name of Jesus Christ. The authority
is complete in man as long as man is in relationship with God
through Jesus Christ. With our authority comes the responsibility to use it for God's purposes. If we don't rebuke the devil, he
will not be rebuked. If we don't drive him back, he will not
leave. It is up to us. Satan knows of our authority, but hopes we
will stay ignorant. We must be as convinced of our authority as
the devil is.

We need to go ahead and exercise our authority in Jesus'
name. For instance, the police in my town have been given legal
authority by the city. It is authority which ordinary citizens do
not have. They wear symbols of their authority: uniforms and
badges. They have their authority all the time, even while
cruising calmly down the road or while parked at a doughnut
shop. Occasionally, however, they are called to the scene of a
crime where they exercise their authority by apprehending an
offender.

What if I were to arrive home and find people stealing my
possessions. I call the police from my car phone and they rush
over to my house. But to my surprise, they line up along the

sidewalk and begin to sing about their authority, declaring it to one another. All the while, intruders finish cleaning out my house! This may seem ridiculous, yet that is often an accurate picture of what we do. We talk about our authority. We sing about it. We even proclaim it loudly. But we don't exercise it. We must recognize that there is a difference between having authority and exercising it.

# Five Methods For Exercising Our Authority

## 1. The Name of Jesus as a Weapon

We need a revelation of what happens among demonic powers when we speak the precious and powerful name of Jesus. It's not a magic word. We must be wholly submitted to Jesus to use it. But this name represents the same Jesus who made demons cry out in terror and beg for a trip into a herd of swine. The name of Jesus has been given to us by the resurrected Son Himself: "In *My name* they will cast out demons" (Mark 16:17, emphasis added). The name of Jesus carries with it all the victory of the Cross and the Resurrection.

## 2. The Word of God in Warfare

The second way to exercise authority is to use the word of God. "And take the helmet of salvation, and the sword of the Spirit, which is the word of God" (Eph. 6:17). The Word of God is not just a book. It is like a sword. It is sharp, two-edged, and has a genuine effect against the enemy. Jesus used the Word of God in the wilderness when dealing with Satan, and we too need to speak out Scripture, using it as a mighty weapon.

One of my first experiences in dealing with demons deeply impressed me with the power of the Bible. I was with Frank Houston, praying for a teenage girl in Australia. The usual voices and strange mutterings confirmed that the girl had at least one demon. Then, instinctively, I quoted I John 3:8 aloud to the demon in the girl:

"The Son of God appeared for this purpose, that He might destroy the works of the devil."

As soon as I quoted that verse, she screamed and spat and screamed again. I was surprised at the demon's volcanic reaction—simply from my quoting a Bible verse.

### 3. The Power of the Holy Spirit

The power of the Holy Spirit is an essential method for exercising our authority. When Jesus breathed on the disciples in John 20:22, saying, "Receive the Holy Spirit," this was the legal authority of the Spirit. He then told them to wait in Jerusalem until they received *dunamis* or "power." "You shall receive power [dunamis] when the Holy Spirit has come upon you; and you shall be My witnesses both in Jerusalem, and in all Judea and Samaria, and even to the remotest part of the earth" (Acts 1:8). *Dunamis* is the ability to carry out authority. A policeman may have the city's authority to enforce the law. However, he also needs the muscle to carry out that authority.

Jesus said in Matthew 12:28, "I cast out demons by the Spirit of God." If He did it by the power of the Holy Spirit, then we also need to "pray at all times in the Spirit" (Eph. 6:18) in order to drive back and break down the powers of the enemy.

### 4. The Blood of Jesus

The fourth way we exercise authority is to remind Satan of the blood of Jesus. "They overcame him [the devil] because of the blood of the Lamb" (Rev. 12:11). We remind Satan of his defeat at the Cross when the precious blood of Jesus was poured out to atone for sin, reversing the curse and the enemy's hold on mankind. The declaration of His blood seems to have a powerful effect on the enemy. It brings that defeat into each and every situation—freshly applying it for this time and place. There really is power in the blood.

### 5. Telling the Truth

The last method through which we can exercise our authority is the word of our testimony. Revelation 12:11 also speaks of overcoming the enemy by our testimony. This means a couple of things. First, it's a declaration of the great acts and character of God. The devil's purpose is to discredit God. He lies to us, telling us God doesn't exist, or that He isn't to be trusted. We defeat his lie by testifying of what God has spoken, how God has moved, what His real character is like, and what great things He has done for us. We proclaim the mighty heart and deeds of God.

Another meaning of the word of our testimony is, to proclaim the truth about ourselves—both negative and positive. When we are honest and open, sharing what is truly in our hearts rather than pretending, we break through darkness into the light. We defeat the work of the enemy who can only function in the darkness of pretense, deception, and hypocrisy. We must always be open, proclaiming the truth, and sharing our hearts and our needs with one another. We must walk in the light.

I've seen people set free and healed just by declaring what was really in their hearts. To stay in balance, however, the positive is equally important. We must proclaim the positive truth about ourselves: who we are in Christ. We can declare to the enemy all the truth of our lives in Him. We can proclaim, "I am washed by Jesus' blood. I am a new creature in Christ. I am acceptable to God as a bride. I am more than a conqueror." This testimony of truth is a mighty weapon. It will shatter the intimidation and accusations of the enemy, which constantly drain our confidence and keep us from exercising our authority.

We must deal with the enemy. He is a defeated foe, but will successfully hold his ground until we exercise our God-given authority against Him.

# CHAPTER NINE

# Why Does a Loving God Allow Evil?

If God is a God of love, why is there evil in the earth? No matter who you are, this is one of the most significant questions you will ever face. It is a crucial question for Christians. When unanswered, it can leave tremendous doubts, or even anger and resentment against God. Some Christians have become overwhelmed at the thought of a good God allowing evil to destroy men. With mounting confusion and frustration, many no longer follow the Lord.

Evil in the world is also one of the great stumbling blocks for non-Christians when they consider God. The French philosopher Charles Baudelaire said, "If there is a God, He must be the devil." When tragedy strikes, God becomes the villain. Unexplained catastrophes are labeled as an "act of God." He is blamed for plague and famine.

Even as Christians, we ask thinly-veiled questions. "Why did my nephew get hit by a car?" "Why did my wife have a stroke?" "Why did I give birth to a deformed child?" "Why did such a good person have to die?" The real question is, "Why did God allow it?" For some it may even be more direct: "Why did God do it?"

Many Christians don't even ask the questions, but simply smolder and fume, all the time trying to maintain a facade of faith. We've been told that to ask these questions is to doubt God, so we go through our lives burning in our hearts because we secretly blame God for our problems and for every calamity.

## We Have to Answer This Question

We can't be good spiritual warriors without having the answer to this question. We can't stand against evil and pray confidently for its removal if we don't know why it's here. We cannot have absolute confidence in God unless we are sure of His innocence when it comes to evil in the earth today.

Many believe that everything that happens is God's will. *Que sera, sera*—whatever will be, will be. They are saying that evil is inevitable. Whatever has happened, is happening, and will happen, must be the will of God. But this is not a Christian concept—it's fatalism. Other religions have this fatalistic view of the world and the will of God. They say, "God's will be done." No matter what happens, it is the will of God.

A friend of mine working in North Africa had a difficult time finding volunteers to plant trees in the desert and to build water catchments. Though this project would benefit many, the people were hesitant, afraid that it might not be God's will to have trees there.

This is not a biblical philosophy. Christianity understands that God has a will which He reveals in His word. People can then choose to obey or disobey (Josh. 24:15; John 3:19-21; Rev. 3:20). Christianity understands that prayer makes a difference in the world. Christianity has an answer to the question of evil in the earth without falsely blaming God for everything.

## We Have Met the Enemy and It Is Us

The first reason evil is in the earth is because of people's choices. Evil, in the moral sense, is not God's fault. If it is God's fault, repentance would be ridiculous and punishment for evil would be unjust.

Romans 5:12 says, "Through one man sin [evil] entered into the world." First, Adam and Eve made their wrong choices with what we call "the fall of man" or "original sin." Since that time we have all endorsed their actions, adding to the evil in the world by our own choices. Billions of people, over thousands of years, making billions upon billions of choices, have advanced evil in the earth to its present state. We have all been willing contributors to evil in the world and should have no difficulty understanding why it is here.

Humanity's present condition is the product of what the Bible refers to as "the curse." The curse is the natural and logical consequences of man's sinful acts.

We are all affected by the sins of others and by evil as it exists in the world. We all die, regardless of our own guilt or innocence. Children are born deformed not because of anyone's sin, but because of the corruption of the world in which we live. Some of the curse is merely inconvenient. Many of us have to wear eyeglasses. Our teeth rot. Our bones break. Some of us spend our lives in wheelchairs. Sometimes terrible things happen. A hundred die because a careless mechanic doesn't repair the plane properly. Herders overgraze their land and thousands of children die in a famine.

Every evil thing has a cause. Sometimes the responsibility is individual. Sometimes it is the result of many people's choices. Sometimes the choices are immoral, other times simply misguided.

As Christians, we struggle with what seems to be God's complicity in all this. We know He is sovereign. Couldn't He step in and do something? Why doesn't He intervene more often? What keeps Him from ending wars, keeping people from tragedy, and instantly making the earth a nice place to live? We made it a mess, but why can't He fix it?

These are not small questions. Left unanswered, these questions greatly affect our faith. There is an answer, however, and that answer is tied directly to how much God loves us.

Evil is allowed to remain in the earth because free will is more valuable than the absence of evil. God created us with free will. Without it we would be less than human. Free will is absolutely necessary for the quality of relationship that God wants us to have with Him and with other human beings.

## Can Puppets Enjoy Love?

God greatly desires to have relationship with us. In fact, the reason God created man was for relationship. Not that He was lonely or bored. There wasn't something lacking in the heart of

God. Man does not complete God. God completes man. God desired a relationship with us, that we might know Him. However, God could not have a relationship with mechanical beings. There would be no meaning if we were mechanical dolls who simply spouted "I love you" when wound up or when our batteries were recharged. We could never know the joy of intimate relationship with our heavenly Father or with others if we, like puppets, only responded to affection with the pull of a string. Freedom to choose to return love, or not to return it, is the basis for relationship.

Free will is more valuable than the absence of evil. How valuable is it? Try to imagine this: Picture a single pile of refuse with all the wars, famines, atrocities, calamities, violence, injustice, selfishness, perversion, hate, and anguish that the world has ever known and ever will know. Try to see the true effect of evil on the world—an immense festering mound of evil. It is far, far beyond what any of us could comprehend. But try to imagine it. Now, go one more step. What if God were to give you the option of ending it right now? If you could rid the world of all evil by removing man's free will, what would you do?

God has already made that very choice. He has said that free will is worth enduring all the evil we have piled together. He would be far more cruel to remove our "human-ness"...our freedom...our free will. The absence of that pile of evil, as foul as it is, is not as valuable as your free will and mine.

Anyone who has been involved in evangelism has tried to answer the question which began this chapter. You may have stood on a street corner or sat in a university classroom, struggling to answer.

"If God is such a loving God, and if He is all powerful, why does He allow evil in the world? Why does He allow innocent babies to die? Why can't He just stop it or protect people from the terrible things of the world?"

These are good questions that deserve equally good answers. They are really a philosophical argument. The argument goes like this: Either God is all-loving but not all-powerful, or

He is all-powerful but not loving. It says that, given the evil in the world, He cannot be both all-powerful and loving.

## Is God Guilty? *HE IS BOTH BUT HE ALSO IS ALL WISE*

While we strain for an appropriate rebuttal, we should consider this: Their argument is absolutely right.

For instance: If I were standing on a street corner and saw a child about to walk out in front of a bus and did nothing to stop her, I would be guilty of negligent homicide. If I had the knowledge and the power to prevent her death and did nothing, I would be guilty. Now, multiply that street corner millions of times. God sees and knows every horrible thing about to happen.

There is much we don't understand about human suffering, and there is certainly much we do not know about God and His infinite wisdom, since God knows everything and we only have finite minds. I do not claim to have all the answers concerning what C.S. Lewis called the "problem with pain." I believe that sometimes we can do nothing except trust His character. Yet even understanding God's character gives us some answers. Even though He has all power, He chooses not to use His omnipotence *because of other equally important factors*. We've looked at one of these factors: the free will He gave to man. And there are others, such as His commitment to justice.

God is just. His justice is without compromise. He is absolutely fair and equitable. He is not arbitrary. Therefore, God cannot stop one war without stopping every war. And He cannot stop one evil without stopping every evil. If God were to stop every evil, He would have to freeze the free will of every living human being, thereby eliminating free will and any chance for us to have true relationship with Him.

Some would say: "Why doesn't God just stop the whole thing? It would be worth it to rid the world of evil." God did that once. He destroyed the whole earth and eliminated every being who was not committed to righteousness—He sent the flood. Only eight people remained. But it was not His final solution.

God is a loving God who is concerned about the condition of the world and the affairs of man. In fact, He is greatly grieved. Every evil, every injustice, every pain, and every tear brings grief to His heart (Isa. 63:10; Ps. 78:40). God cannot, and never has, merely sat back and allowed evil to flourish. God's love compels Him to become involved. He has never stopped acting to counteract evil. God's power enables Him to do whatever is necessary. But His sense of justice compels Him to limit His power, to not overstep the freedom He gave man (Matt. 23:37; Prov. 1:24; Isa. 65:1-3).

God is not only loving, all-powerful, and just; He is also wise. God's wisdom has made a way for man, in man's own free will, to choose a way out of the bondage and suffering of the world and into relationship with Him. God's powerful, loving, just, and wise solution was Jesus and the Cross (John 3:16).

### It Isn't Going to Last Forever

In God's wisdom, He is able to see the temporal nature of our suffering. No man has to endure evil or suffering for long. The duration of life on Planet Earth is insignificant in light of eternity. Man's suffering is equally insignificant in light of an eternal relationship with God. God has made a way for man to know freedom, peace, and life in his heart and spirit. That is greater than any suffering he endures in a world of turmoil, or through affliction in his body. God has made a way for man to escape the consequences of his own selfishness—to escape the evil he has brought upon himself. It is up to man to choose life or death. Man can live in temporal suffering and eternal life, or in eternal suffering and eternal death. No one has to suffer forever unless he or she chooses to.

We have seen that evil remains in the earth because free will is more valuable than its absence. God has chosen to deal with evil through man's free will, not in spite of it. He continues to work toward restoration of relationship with Him and the final, complete removal of evil in the world.

## Be an Overcomer, Not a Casualty

There is another reason why evil is in the earth. It is also for man's development. The fact that man has brought evil into the world has not escaped God: Evil is here by man's choice. But God is willing to use the presence of evil and the fallen state of man's world to develop a people who will rise above and combat evil. This is why the Bible so often uses the word "overcome." We are to be "overcomers."

If we are to overcome, we must first become fully aware of what an evil, selfish world we live in. We are not exempt from daily life in a fallen world. Evil and selfishness are in operation everywhere and at all times. We are continually exposed to, and suffer the consequences of, life in a fallen world. We shouldn't be overwhelmed by the selfishness of people. Evil should come as no surprise. We should not be shaken. We should learn to expect it and refuse to be unsettled because of it (Heb. 11:24-26).

God uses evil in the world to develop us in two ways: first, as a battlefield in our lives. God doesn't intend for us to be casualties by becoming confused, angry, or resentful. Neither does He want us to hide our heads in the sand and pretend evil isn't all around us. He wants us to allow what is taking place on this planet to develop our lives, without letting it overtake us. The world is what it is, and the choice is ours. We can either let it strengthen us and increase our resolve to make a difference in the world, or we can let it weaken us and become a casualty of the war.

God uses the fallen world to develop us through trials, testings, and tribulations. We need to understand that there are such things as tests, trials, and tribulations. We could pretend they don't exist. Some religions teach that we must view evil as an "illusion." Even some Christians have said we should not make a "negative confession," lest bad things happen to us. But bad things are real, and some don't go away. If we pray and things are still bad, we can choose to let those circumstances develop us. We don't have to like them. But we also don't have to let them rob us of victory. We don't always have victory from things, but we can always have victory in things. Victory is in the heart. Victory is being an overcomer in every situation.

If we are armed with a realistic expectation of tests, trials, and temptations, we will not be overwhelmed and overtaken by them. Don't shake your head and say, "Why is this happening to me?" Instead, determine to grow and develop as a direct result of less-than-perfect situations. That is victory.

I hear story after story of needless casualties. Churches split. Financial crises destroy ministries. Pastors run off with young women. People are shocked and disillusioned. They begin to doubt and even blame God. Some fall away and stop serving God. This happens not just to the weak, but to those who have seen miracles, have been involved in powerful ministries, and have seen tremendous evidence of God's faithfulness.

### Victory Isn't Living Behind Bulletproof Glass

The problem is, these people have never faced the undeniable fact that we live in a fallen world. They think victory is exclusion from tests, trials, and temptations. They have concocted a fantasy world where salvation means exemption from the terrible things. They are totally unprepared when reality invades their lives.

To the degree we have accepted the reality of the fallen world in which we live, and to the degree that we are determined to use it to develop us, we can have victory in our lives.

> *Beloved, do not be surprised at the fiery ordeal among you, which comes upon you for your testing, as though some strange thing were happening to you; but to the degree that you share the sufferings of Christ, keep on rejoicing; so that also at the revelation of His glory, you may rejoice with exultation (I Peter 4:12-13).*

Peter wrote his letters to Christians who were being daily delivered up for persecution and death. They read his letters while waiting to be torn apart by lions in the Colosseum. Some read these words before being dipped in oil and set ablaze as torches for the emperor's parties. Peter told them that nothing we go through as Christians has anything to do with our relationship with God. And he told them to rejoice in the midst of terrible circumstances.

## Either We're Crazy or We Know Something

We live in a fallen world. God lets things happen. We should not be surprised when they do. The only way we can rejoice in the midst of tribulation is if we are crazy, or if we know enough about God, about the Word of God, and about the condition of man and our planet.

In a previous verse, Peter said we are to glorify God through everything we do and say. Through our actions and reactions, every hour and in every situation, we are revealing God's glory—His character—to those around us. If we know His character, we can come to the end of each experience rejoicing, knowing that nothing we'll ever encounter can throw us off our course. If we know God, we know His love for us is the same. His kind intentions toward us and His purposes for us have not changed. In the midst of every disappointment, we can rejoice, because God in us is victorious. And the character of God will be shown to others as we face our trials.

> *Consider it all joy, my brethren, when you encounter various trials; knowing that the testing of your faith produces endurance. And let endurance have its perfect result, that you may be perfect and complete, lacking in nothing (James 1:2-4).*

"Various trials," and "the testing of your faith," are not joys. We must consider them joy. We can go through times of turmoil, when we can barely handle the physical, mental, and emotional pain, and we can say, "This is a joy." Why? Because terrible, fiery ordeals are producing something of unparalleled value in our lives: endurance.

We know little about endurance in the Western world. Our society demands convenience and comfort. If we don't like something, we change it. However, the majority of people have no opportunity to change their situation in life. They simply learn to endure.

Without exception, we are all going to have trials. Those who learn to endure are victors. We can't put a price on endurance. It is one of the most valuable things we can have.

Endurance is going through what life brings us with joy in our hearts. If we could see what God sees, we would realize the wealth that comes with endurance. We would truly be joyful in the midst of every situation.

Jesus did not die on the Cross that we might avoid life, but that we might be overcomers. He gives us grace for every situation. Jesus lived a sinless life, went to the Cross, died a painful death, went to hell, ripped authority and the power of sin, death, and Hades from Satan, rose from the dead, ascended to the right hand of the Father, and is there interceding for us every minute of every day. If this is not enough proof of God's love for us, if this can't help us endure any situation and become all that we need to be, we had better start looking for a new religion.

How can we be perfect, complete, and lacking in nothing? By simply enduring. And while enduring say, "This is a joy to me." This isn't psyching ourselves up or defrauding our minds. It is just recognizing that each situation is developing us—that we really are becoming like Jesus who, with joy, endured far more than any of us ever will.

God is always there for us. He is always turning things around to be a blessing and a benefit for us. This is what Romans 8:28 means. He is always working in the circumstances that come our way to bring about our good. We need only endure and let endurance have its perfect result.

Let's look carefully into Romans chapter 5 to see how it works:

> *Therefore having been justified by faith, we have peace with God through our Lord Jesus Christ, through whom also we have obtained our introduction by faith into this grace in which we stand; and we exult in hope of the glory of God. And not only this, but we also exult in our tribulations; knowing that tribulation brings about perseverance; and perseverance, proven char-*

*acter; and proven character, hope; and hope does not disappoint; because the love of God has been poured out within our hearts through the Holy Spirit who was given to us (Rom. 5:1-3).*

## Wholeheartedly Embracing Disappointment

What does it mean to "exult in our tribulations"? It's not avoiding them, or pretending they don't exist. It's not resisting every negative thing that comes into our lives. It's not even gritting our teeth in quiet submission to our circumstances. Exulting in our tribulations is a wholehearted embrace of every unwanted situation, unbearable turmoil, and disappointment. To exult is to rejoice completely in the midst of tribulation; not in spite of tribulation, but because of it. To the world this would seem insane. But it is the most reasonable thing we can do if we understand what immeasurable benefit tribulation is to us.

There is no greater witness in the world than that of a Christian who endures, who truly exults in and overcomes everything the world and the devil can throw at him. Making these things work for us and not against us is real spiritual warfare.

Note also in Romans 5:4-5 that perseverance brings about "proven character." This is God's goal for each of us. God allows us to go through trials that we might all have proven character. Proven character brings about hope and "hope does not disappoint" because we know we can make it through anything. We have been there and have confidence.

God is not unconcerned about us. He is building us up—making us strong, mature, and more like Jesus. There is never a moment when God is not working in us. This is the reason we can exult in our tribulations.

*And you shall remember all the way which the Lord your God has led you in the wilderness these forty years, that He might humble you, testing you, to know what was in your heart, whether you would keep His commandments or not (Deut. 8:2).*

God leading Israel into the wilderness is more than a historical fact. There are also many lessons from these events to teach how He deals with us.

For Israel the wilderness was a very real place. It presented daily hazards and kept them from even the simple comforts they once knew as slaves. The wilderness was by no means a nice place. It was not a place of rest and refreshment. It was a place where energy was drained by the hot sun and the harshness of the desert winds. It was a place where food and water were scarce.

## Wilderness Born and Bred

The wilderness was a place of death, as an entire generation grew weak and perished there. Along with them perished the grumbling, bitterness, fear, and frailty. The wilderness was also a place of life, where an entire generation was born and nurtured. This new generation became the conquering warriors of Israel. They were strong and brave, with characters tempered by the wilderness. Knowing nothing but the poverty of the wilderness and its utter lack of comfort, they sought to gain the promises of God.

God knew exactly what He was doing when He sent them into the wilderness. And today God continues to do the same for His people. Our wilderness is not one of sand dunes and water holes, but it is equally real. Our wilderness experiences are part of living in a fallen world. Without exception, we all go through them.

There are many wildernesses in life. If we don't understand why God is allowing us to go through them, we will become frustrated and bitter toward God. This is particularly true if we have been taught that with enough faith we will not go through them. If we believe this, not only will we go through wildernesses, but we will condemn ourselves for lack of faith. Or we may blame God for breaking His promises. Jesus overcame the enemy in the inconvenient circumstances of the desert. We must also face our wildernesses, overcoming them and revealing the victory of Christ in practical life.

Why does God lead us into the wilderness? First, to humble us. During these times, we remember who we are and who God is. It is always humbling to be in the wilderness. It makes us more dependent. Being in the wilderness also puts a spotlight on our lives. Others take notice of our situation and it is humbling to admit we are going through hard times.

You may find this uncomfortable; our world has taught us to avoid any humbling. But God knows that the greatest thing we can have is consistent humility. We should never try to escape the wilderness or avoid the humbling. Humility is good; it is pride we should fear. We should remain faithful, trust God, endure, and be grateful for humbling experiences.

## Being Road Tested

The second reason God leads us into the wilderness is to be tested. When we buy a car, we can be relatively certain that it will last because it has been tested for defects, safety, and roadworthiness. In fact, the tests performed on it were far more rigorous than any car would face during regular use.

God tests us in much the same way. He allows us to be in situations that reveal the content of our character. Under pressure, that which is in us comes out. Testing reveals our weaknesses and strengths to God and to us. God wants to repair our faults in the factory rather than out on the roadway of ministry.

Only in the wilderness will we know the contents of our hearts. We can sit in Sunday morning services, sing songs, and pray prayers for 40 years. But if we avoid the wilderness, we may never know what is in us.

As we face situations not to our liking, when we are deprived, or when things are out of control, we will be astonished at what surfaces. We can respond in a number of ways: We can feel uncomfortable, become angry, and complain. We can blame others. The more pride we have, the more difficult it will be to see what comes out of our hearts. In pride we can deny the attitudes, emotions, and reactions that emerge; or in humility, we can accept what we see and deal with it responsibly.

# What to Do in the Wilderness

- Truly thank the Lord for showing you the things in your heart.

- Repent, asking God to forgive any sin or wrong motives. You may also need to ask others to forgive you.

- Seek God's help to overcome and create new habits and attitudes.

- Resist the enemy in his attempts in your life.

- Never deny that you are going through a wilderness experience.

- Never feel condemned for that which has surfaced during your wilderness experience.

- Simply say, "Thank you, God, for showing me what was in my heart. Now I'll do something about it."

Satan's condemnation paralyzes because it's general and vague. But the conviction of the Holy Spirit is specific and can be dealt with immediately. The conviction of the Spirit leads to freedom if we repent and ask forgiveness.

## Why Are So Many Leaders Falling?

God is looking for leaders. If the Body of Christ lacks anything, it lacks secure, mature, and consistent leaders. We don't need more positions filled. We need leaders who lead in humility and strength. Satan has launched an awesome attack on leaders in every level of society. From pastors to politicians to parents, they are falling every day. When a leader falls, the consequences are horrendous. But fallen leaders were not necessarily the wrong ones to lead. Perhaps they were never properly tested in the wilderness. Perhaps fame and fortune or their own theology kept them from tests that would have strengthened and established them, or exposed them as unprepared for leadership.

Thousands of individuals are not surviving because they believe they have a God-given right to escape the wilderness. They wake up one morning to find themselves in the midst of a most unexpected wilderness and they fall apart. God wants leaders who will willingly stand and be tested by the wilderness. The greater a person's potential for leadership, the greater the tests he or she will face.

As you read this, I can unreservedly promise you leadership. I cannot promise you a title, but I can promise you leadership. If you give yourself to developing Christian character, if you go through the tests and prove yourself, the world will beat a path to your door, regardless of your gifts, background, or personality. They will want what you have. You will lead them to Christ by your example. The Church needs those who will allow God to develop them so that they will stand up in the heat of the battle and not betray nor disappoint those who look to them for strength and stability.

We all go through wilderness experiences to see whether or not we will keep God's commandments. It is almost always in the wilderness that we blow it—that's where we fall. The wilderness is where we have a tendency toward certain sins, where it is easier to move in the wrong direction. If we are prone to lust, we will lust in the wilderness. It will be a time when we are tempted to quit, to fail, to sin, and to step out of the will of God.

God sends us through these times not to fail, but to prevail. If we can remain faithful and obedient, keeping His commandments in the wilderness, we will excel in every situation. This is God's desire for each of us. If we continue to obey Him in difficult times, we are truly committed. However, if we cannot keep His commandments in the wilderness, we are not really committed.

The wilderness is one of the best places for us to grow. When we go through wildernesses, resisting sin, obeying God, and withstanding every temptation, then we truly have character and are growing spiritually. But even if we blow it, we shouldn't give up. We should repent, humble ourselves, and determine again to overcome by God's grace. We should never let the enemy force us out of the wilderness school.

# CHAPTER TEN

## Deliver Us From Evil

I was just a young missionary, but I was shocked at what the older pastor was telling me. I met him in a small town high in the mountains.

"I moved out of the city, Dean," he explained. He went on to tell how he had once been in charge of a thriving ministry in a major city. "But the city was just too evil...not a place to live for the Lord at all," he continued. "There was just too much pressure to sin."

I was dumbfounded. This pastor had taken many of his church people and retreated to the mountains to escape temptation. Now that city had a little less salt and light. However, I'm sure the Christians weren't able to leave sin behind. They just found new temptations. Temptation is a part of life, no matter where you live.

We can't blame our neighborhood, nor our circumstances for temptation. Neither can we blame God. According to James 1:13-15:

> Let no one say when he is tempted, "I am being tempted by God"; for God cannot be tempted by evil, and He Himself does not tempt any one. But each one is tempted when he is carried away and enticed by his own lust. Then when lust has conceived, it gives birth to sin; and when sin is accomplished, it brings forth death.

There is hope, though.

*No temptation has overtaken you but such as is common to man; and God is faithful, who will not allow you to be tempted beyond what you are able; but with the temptation will provide the way of escape also, that you may be able to endure it (I Cor. 10:13).*

This verse teaches us a number of important things about temptation. The Bible shows us that temptation is not sin. Many people feel dirty and suffer tremendous guilt because they have been tempted, but temptation is not a sin. Hebrews 4:15 says that Jesus was "tempted in all things as we are, yet without sin." If temptation carries guilt, then Jesus was guilty. The difference between sin and temptation is this: Temptation is considering sin; it becomes sin when we commit ourselves to it. Sin may not be an act—it can also be a thought that we dwell on in our minds. We need a revelation from God to show us that we can be greatly tempted without being dirtied.

Temptation, according to I Corinthians, can "overtake" us. This means that temptations are external to us. They are outside of the "new creation" that we are in Christ.

Second Corinthians 5:17 says, "Therefore if any man is in Christ, he is a new creature; the old things passed away; behold, new things have come." What does it means to be a new creature? It means that sin is no longer a part of who we are. If we say, "I am a thief," or, "I am a liar," we will never conquer these sins. The devil will provoke us to sin because we believe it is part of who we are. Satan will say, "You're just like that. You've had this problem for 30 years. This is your weakness." Instead of believing his lies, we must believe the Bible when it says we have become new.

**You Aren't The Only One**

Another fact is: Temptation is also common to man, according to the verse in I Corinthians. Everyone is tempted. We need never feel alone in our struggles with temptation. Many believe they alone have evil thoughts. I have counseled people who say, "I know I'm the only one who has this trouble. I start to have my quiet time and all of a sudden, all these terrible thoughts fill my mind!" Such relief comes when I tell such people, "No, you're not the only one. Actually I've counseled several this week who've said the same thing."

This is why appropriate public confession and humbling are so beneficial for the Body of Christ. When someone confesses a sin, there are many who are encouraged, knowing that they are not alone. We need to be more honest with each other and share our burdens, our difficulties, and our temptations.

I am thankful for the close, loyal friends I work with in Youth With A Mission. We have been encouraged to be accountable to each other over the years and share our struggles. This helps save us from many pitfalls.

Some believe that a spiritual person does not experience temptation. This isn't true. The truly mature man or woman of God readily confesses struggles with temptation. On the other hand, the devil loves to tell us individually how perverted and different we are. He tells us we are the only person doing what we do. Others have found freedom from sin in Christ, but we are unique and hopeless. We will never be free. These too are lies from the enemy. The temptations we experience are common to Christians throughout the world, and their power over us can be diminished.

There is not only the sin itself, but the power behind it urging and encouraging us toward it. Even if we say "no," we haven't dealt with the power. We deal with the provoking powers behind temptations by humbling ourselves and becoming open before God and man. Then our prayers can block these driving powers.

A friend of mine in full-time ministry was strongly tempted by homosexuality. Most of the time he overcame, but the urges were always there. He didn't get victory until he confessed his struggles to a select group of trusted friends. They prayed for him and accepted him in love. Since this time of humbling himself, he has walked free of the powerful drive behind this sin.

We may secretly hope that there will come a time when we will "arrive" and live in victory without temptation. We think temptation is keeping us from being what God wants us to be. But the absence of temptation would never make us better

Christians. Unless we can find victory in the midst of temptation, we have no victory at all.

## Sin Is Not Inevitable

If we believe the lies of Satan when he tells us we are inevitably going to sin and that temptation is too strong for us, then we will sin. If we believe we have no chance against it, we are doomed. But I Corinthians 10:13 shows us that temptation is never more than we can bear. We must know beyond any doubt that God's Word is true when He says He won't allow us to be tempted beyond our ability to resist.

With God's grace, we are able to resist temptation to the point of victory. Thousands of Christians are continually falling into sin because they don't have a revelation of the new creation that they are in Christ. We need to speak to the devil and say, "Sin shall not have dominion over me" (Rom. 6:14 KJV).

The Bible is clear that we can live an overcoming life (Rev.12:11). If this were not true, where is the power of the Cross and the Resurrection to keep us free from sin? If sin were inevitable, the term "new creation" would be only words, because nothing is really new at all.

> *Consider yourselves to be dead to sin, but alive to God in Christ Jesus. Therefore do not let sin reign in your mortal body that you should obey its lusts, and do not go on presenting the members of your body to sin as instruments of unrighteousness; but present yourselves to God as those alive from the dead, and your members as instruments of righteousness to God. For sin shall not be master over you, for you are not under law, but under grace (Rom. 6:11-14).*

Let us concentrate more on the righteousness of God within us than on the potential of sin. This is not the so-called doctrine of sinless perfection. No one but Jesus was sinless on earth. Until we go to heaven, we will always be correcting and changing our attitudes, motives, and actions. But with the aid of the Holy Spirit, we should be becoming more like Jesus every day. Sin should be rarer and rarer as we grow in Him. He is able to keep us from stumbling and to make us stand in His presence blameless with great joy (Jude 24).

### There's Always An Escape Hatch

First Corinthians 10:13 promises us that God will always provide a way of escape from temptation. What is this "way of escape"? A better question might be: *Who* is this way of escape? The life of Joseph is a wonderful study in how to escape temptation. Throughout his life, he was tempted but overcame. The most graphic temptation came while he was working for Mr. Potiphar. After a period of time, Mrs. Potiphar took a liking to Joseph, and suggested to him one day, "Come and lie with me." This was not only a sexual temptation, but it was the most logical thing to do. To do anything else was career suicide. If he had just kept her happy, he would have it made. Had Joseph only been considering his own position and life, he might have given in. He certainly must have been aware of the consequences of rejecting Mrs. Potiphar. Still, he did not fall.

Joseph said to Mrs. Potiphar: "How can I sin against God and do this evil thing?" Joseph lived in the fear of the Lord. He escaped temptation because he considered God's reaction to the situation.

If we are only concerned about whether we'll get caught or what others will think, and if we only consider our needs, our rights, our desires, our suffering, or anything other than the heart of God, we will not escape temptation. We must live in the fear of God. Consider the heart of God. Ask for the fear of the Lord which, according to Proverbs is "to hate evil" (Prov. 8:13 KJV).

Jesus taught us to pray regularly: "Lead us not into temptation, but deliver us from evil...." As God leads our lives, He can help us escape heavy temptation.

### Direct Attack

God sometimes allows us to be attacked by the enemy. This doesn't mean that the devil can steal our salvation, make us sin, or possess us against our will.

Consider what Paul said: "For this reason, to keep me from exalting myself, there was given me a thorn in the flesh, a messenger of Satan to buffet me—to keep me from exalting myself" (II Cor. 12:7). Here was Paul, a Spirit-filled believer, being buffeted by a messenger of Satan. Every Christian has and will experience the attack of the enemy. Most of the time God allows this because He wants us to learn to resist.

We need to learn to rise up and resist Satan's assaults. Most of the time, these attacks are only for a time, such as in the case of Job. In some rare cases, like that of Paul's, God allows the attack to continue, knowing that His grace is enough for anyone. However, we are never meant to passively accept whatever the devil throws our way. If we do not learn to resist him, he will climb all over us—sometimes for years—until we stand against him.

## Five Ways Satan Attacks Us

"Therefore I am well content with weaknesses [infirmities], with insults [reproaches], with distresses, with persecutions, with difficulties, for Christ's sake; for when I am weak, then I am strong" (II Cor. 12:10). There are many ways the devil attacks us. Second Corinthians 12:10 lists five of the most common ways: infirmities, reproaches, distresses, persecutions, and difficulties.

### 1. Infirmities

This simply means that the devil can attack us physically. If we do not realize this, he may consistently afflict us in our bodies.

This is not to say that every sickness is from the devil. There are two extreme positions in the Body of Christ regarding this. One group holds that all sickness is from the devil. This is not true, unless we mean that all sickness came into the world because of the fall of man. The other camp is committed to the belief that no sickness is ever from the devil. It is just a scientific reality with which we must deal. This is equally untrue.

Sickness can be caused by germs. Most often, we are sick not because of the devil, nor because of sin in our lives, nor because of judgment from God. We are sick from bacteria, viruses, or physiological abnormalities. This is the world in which we live. We may be sick because of inherent weaknesses. For instance, just because I wear glasses doesn't mean I have a demon. Our bodies are finite and break down. Frailty has been passed down through the human family ever since the Fall.

Sickness can also be the result of abuse to our bodies. Improper diet, lack of exercise, or lack of rest may bring illness.

Occasionally, though, sickness can come from a supernatural source. It can be an act of God. I used to preach that God would never bring sickness on His children. But I read the Bible and found that sometimes He did. God occasionally uses sickness as a physical judgment. When He does, it is a merciful act to bring about repentance and restoration. If a sickness is from God and a person repents, there is almost always an immediate recovery.

Once while ministering in New Guinea, a young man with us developed a mysterious fever that lasted over four weeks. We prayed constantly for him and obtained medical attention. But even though we saw others healed during this time, neither our prayers nor the medicine had any effect on this young man. Then one day he confessed some terrible bitterness he had harbored in his heart. He was instantly healed without a prayer being said for him.

Another supernatural source of sickness can be the devil. We need to resist his attacks. Say something like this: "Satan, I refuse to accept this attack. I command you in Jesus' Name to leave me alone!" If we are uncertain whether or not it is an attack from Satan, we need to ask God. He will be faithful to show us the source of the problem. Whatever the cause, we should always press into God for understanding and healing.

## 2. Reproaches

Satan attacks through reproaches. They are Satan's attempts to make us look bad. The world keeps a close eye on the Church of Jesus Christ. If there is ever a reason to condemn, Satan will ensure the reproach of the Church. Sadly, many believers help the devil bring reproach, either by their own sin or by their constant suspicions and slander of other Christians.

The media will be the first to proclaim our unfaithfulness, our scandals, our infidelity. The world will try to link Christians with every bizarre cult or hypocritical religious leader. Resist the enemy and refuse to be a part of his attacks to bring reproaches. One way to block him is to resist temptation yourself. Before you give in and sin, think of the way Satan is trying to make you the cause of reproach. Also, blunt Satan's attacks on others by refusing to pass on slander and gossip. If you're involved in publishing books or magazine articles, be especially careful not to attack brothers and sisters in Christ.

### 3. Distresses

The powers of darkness can attack us by influencing us toward distress. As circumstances and relationships come under siege, we are always tempted to become distressed instead of remaining full of faith. The enemy brings us into despair and panic, hoping we will give up. There is incredible pressure to quit, to drop out, to burn out, or to feel we can't cope with life or ministry.

### 4. Persecutions

Satan also attacks through persecution. He will hinder the preaching of the Gospel by persecuting the preachers. History is full of martyrdom, imprisonments, and every conceivable method of hindrance—all to keep the Gospel from being proclaimed. Satan also uses persecution to prevent people from continuing as committed Christians.

### 5. Difficulties

Lastly, Satan can attack by holding back our necessities, or in the words of II Corinthians 12:10, by sending "difficulties" our way. The acquiring of things needed to get the Gospel out to the lost is being hindered by the powers of darkness. This is a major strategy of the enemy to discredit God and His faithfulness, and to keep His work from going forward. Unfortunately, it is amazingly successful. How many missionaries and pastors have given up, disillusioned after years of battling severe financial hardship? We have to resist the enemy, and see the release of finances, buildings, workers, and all the provisions we need for ministry. We must resist the devil until he quits. He is hoping that we will quit first.

## It's Time to Stop Him

The devil gets away with whatever we let him. This does not mean that he will give up easily. He knows human nature and is relying on our lack of endurance, hoping we will give up first, as we often do. If we continue to resist him he will finally give up. It may not be immediate, but it will happen. The more determined we are, the less determined he is. If we are convinced that we have the authority, he will see it and eventually cease his attack. We should never give in or become discouraged. Victory is ours, but the price is faith and persistence.

We live in a fallen world. Evil is all around us, but Christ is within us. We will continue to experience things we would rather avoid. If we respond the right way, they will develop us. There are no shortcuts to strength or character. We are tested that we might develop character. We are subject to temptation that we might become strong and develop a hatred for evil. We are attacked by Satan that we might increase our dependence on God and develop spiritual muscle. God is calling us to stop being victims and become mighty warriors in all of life's realities.

# CHAPTER ELEVEN

# Does Prayer Really Change Things?

There is a battle going on. It is fierce and hot. The theater of this war is us. We are the battlefield. Immense forces are clashing, waging war for our individual souls. We are also being developed as warriors. We are to fight not only for ourselves, but for every other victim of Satan's attacks. We must be spiritual warriors for the Kingdom at large.

The world we live in is greatly contaminated by evil. According to the Bureau of Crime Statistics in Washington, D.C., in 1988 there was one murder every 25 minutes in the United States. One American woman is raped every five minutes. Every 60 seconds a child is abused, and each year two thousand children are killed by their own parents. Every day bullets, bombs, fires, and drunk drivers take innocent lives. People steal, lie, and defraud. Governments exploit and oppress. Elected officials and trusted men of stature slink off to do unspeakable things. Our children are preyed upon by drugs, pornography, homosexuality, suicide, and the occult. Millions of people passively wait for disease and famine to rob them of life.

## Retreating in Panic or Flailing in Fury

It's simply too much to take in. Some react by retreating, trying to ignore the world and only think pleasant thoughts. These folks build walls of pretense around their lives to insulate them from the real world. Many have chosen this route, ignoring the death and destruction around them. They can be happy and content, surrounded by art and music, avoiding the bad parts of town, and not listening to the news lest they become too depressed.

The opposite reaction is to lash out against evil, jumping into the fray in unreasoning fury. These folks see the great injustices even if they don't understand their true source. In great despair, anger, and bitterness, they determine to do something, anything. They embrace humanism, the New Age movement, Marxism...anything that claims to radically combat the conditions of the world.

Even Christians can take action in the wrong way. Many well-meaning folks give money, time, and efforts to improve man's situation, but ignore the spiritual way to combat evil. They are more concerned with man's condition than with God's heart. They attend protests, organize boycotts, or launch educational efforts, but spend little or no time in prayer, spiritual warfare, or evangelism.

There is a middle ground between these two extremes. We don't have to retreat from pain, nor flail about in frantic activity. We can come to a place where we are not overwhelmed by the realities of the planet on which we live. We can be aware of the sin in the world and do something truly effective to stop it. We can be developed as warriors for the advancement of the Kingdom of God. This is why God has left us here.

Mature Christianity begins by knowing what God has done for you, and knowing who you are in Christ. This is foundational, but it is not enough. We are never mature until we accept our responsibilities to advance the Kingdom of God. We are here to fight, and the sooner we learn this, the sooner we move toward mature Christianity. It's not just what God has done for us, but what we do through God as warriors.

## Defense and Offense

As warriors, we take up both defensive and offensive positions. Every football team has a defensive mode. They do all they can to prevent the other team from penetrating their side of the field. A good defensive team keeps opponents from pushing past them. The same is true of spiritual warfare.

Ephesians 6:10-11 says, "Finally, be strong in the Lord, and in the strength of His might. Put on the full armor of God, that you may be able to stand firm against the schemes of the devil."

Standing firm is our defense of righteousness and truth. When we are committed to righteousness and truth, we must defend them in our lives and in the broader arena, in society.

There is also an offensive position. Again, like the offense of a football team, we not only want to hold our ground, but push into our opponent's end zone. We want to penetrate his defenses. Unfortunately, many operate only in the defensive mode spiritually. Their highest goal is for the game to end in a tie. Unwilling to take new ground for God, they only hope the devil doesn't make any points either.

### The Gates of Hell Are Prevailing

We go to church, meeting after meeting, and continually hear that God is building His Church. We hear that the Church is mighty and "the gates of hell shall not prevail against it." We say "Amen, isn't that wonderful!" But the sad truth is, the gates of Hell *are* prevailing. Entire cities, colleges, high schools, clubs, families, marriages, and individuals are trapped behind the gates of hell.

The Bible does not say the gates of hell will automatically fall down. Gates are a defensive weapon. If there is no attack, they will continue to stand. The gates of hell are not going to fall down by themselves. A strong, mature Body of Christ must go on the offense. We have to move against them. When we advance against the gates of hell, then they will not prevail (Matt. 16:18 KJV). We go on the offense by putting on the full armor of God and standing firm against the schemes of the devil.

The Bible meticulously records events in the history of Israel for us to learn spiritual truths from them. We can learn how to go on the offense for God from their experiences fighting for the Promised Land.

*Now these are the nations which the Lord left, to test Israel by them (that is, all who had not experienced*

*any of the wars of Canaan; only in order that the*
*generations of the sons of Israel might be taught war,*
*those who had not experienced it formerly) (Jud. 3:1).*

God delivered Israel from bondage in Egypt. This very real, historical event is very much like our salvation. When we are saved, we are brought out of bondage. When God led Israel through the Red Sea, we can liken that to our baptism. When God took them into the wilderness, they were to be tested, tempted, attacked, and finally renewed, strengthened, and purified. This also correlates well with the Christian experience. God brought the Israelites into the wilderness to discover whether or not they had what it takes to be the people of God. They didn't. God then used the wilderness to produce another generation. Finally after 40 years, a people emerged mature enough, committed enough, and strong enough to be trusted to enter into the Promised Land.

## Enemies in the Promised Land

God led them through the Jordan with another supernatural act and they came into the Promised Land. Almost five hundred years after God had spoken to Abraham, they were finally in their homeland, a land flowing with milk and honey.

What an incredible time of celebration it must have been! They must have expected a time of peace, prosperity, and ease. But when the jubilation died down and they looked around, they discovered they were not alone in their Promised Land. The Promised Land was full of hostile, warlike tribes who worshiped strange gods. And they weren't going to hand the Israelites the keys to their cities, either.

Israel may have wondered if they were in the right land. Did God fail in His promise to them? Weren't they done with striving? Where was the rest? Who were these strangers, and why did God allow them to remain in the Promised Land?

God did not fail. The Promised Land was exactly as it should have been. Judges 3:1 tells us God purposely left hostile nations to develop Israel as warriors. Not that God set up these nations as punching bags, either; these groups justly deserved punishment. But God didn't judge them supernaturally, as He

did Sodom and Gomorrah. Instead, He left them for the Israelites to deal with. They needed to learn to fight.

## We Have to Fight

This is exactly what happens with every Christian: Salvation brings us into the Promised Land, but we must learn to be
spiritual warriors. We must deal with our own "hostile tribes."

The Bible teaches us that unless we drive out the tribes, they
will not be driven out. And unless we rely on God, we will not
be able to drive them out. The very presence of these tribes kept
the people of God completely dependent on Him. God was
telling Israel, and continues to tell us today, that if we are
uncompromisingly obedient to Him, we need never lose a battle
or forfeit our rest in Him.

Just like the children of Israel, our Promised Land is complete. God has done to the devil all that He is going to do on this
earth. The rest is up to us. We are to drive out the powers of
darkness. We cannot do it without God. And God will not do it
apart from us. This is the way it is on Planet Earth. We must
learn to be warriors. We have to learn to rely on God. If we
consistently walk in obedience before God, we need never lose
a battle. But we will do the actual fighting.

If I as a father discover a mess my children have made, it
won't do them any good if I clean it up for them. They will only
develop responsibility if I make them clean it up. We have made
a mess in the earth through our sin. Our heavenly Father has
wisely said that although He will help us, we must clean it up.

God is telling us that we have responsibility. He will do it
through us, but not in spite of us. We are to evangelize. We are
to pray. We are to resist the devil. If we do not resist the devil,
he will not be resisted. Filled with God's Holy Spirit, in the name
of Jesus Christ, with His infinite grace, and power, we can
become effective warriors. If we are waiting around for God to
do it all, we are waiting in vain. This is not the way He operates
in the earth. Much of what He does is through His people. He
has told us what to do and has given us the weapons to use.

# The Weapons He Has Given Us

How do we wage spiritual warfare? The primary method is through intercession. "First of all, then, I urge that entreaties and prayers, petitions and thanksgivings, be made on behalf of all men" (I Tim. 2:1).

When Paul wrote to Timothy, "First of all," he put prayer as the top priority for the Church. Prayer is simply communion with God—conversing with Him, and listening for His encouragement and direction. Every significant event and movement in church history was brought to birth in prayer. From the apostle Paul to John Wesley to Billy Graham, influence on the earth has been proportionate to the influence the Church has had on her knees. Prayer for all Christians must be "first of all."

## Petitioning

One type of prayer Paul mentions in I Timothy 2 is "petitioning." Petitions are simply requests made to God. Supplications are continuous petitions. Many of us have heard preachers say, "God gets sick of our asking." But there is no place in the Bible where God frowns on our asking. In fact, it is a command of God. He encourages it. He is a giving God who wants the best for us. We need to learn to ask with the right motives, but we should always feel free to ask God.

## Thanksgivings

Paul also includes prayers of "thanksgivings." These are prayers that acknowledge with faith that God is God and that He is working in us, through us, and for us. We should confidently declare that He will do what we have asked Him to do: *Thank You Lord; You will do it. Thank You Lord; You are just. Thank You Lord; You are able to do exceedingly, abundantly above all we can ask or think.*

Every request we have of God is to be made with continual thanksgiving. Every prayer of thanksgiving launches another arrow into Satan's camp, much like every complaint and confession of unbelief draws an arrow into ours.

## Entreaties

When Paul speaks of "entreaties," or intercession, as a type of prayer, it means two things. It is firstly, ministry and prayer "on behalf of." Jesus is the great intercessor and our example when it comes to intercession. He lived a sinless life on our behalf. He died on the Cross on our behalf. He lives every day to intercede on our behalf (Heb. 7:25). His life, death, and resurrection were acts of intercession. He is at this very moment interceding before the Father for us.

Secondly, entreaties or intercession mean to "come between." There is always an outside object for intercession. We can't intercede for ourselves. We can intercede for other individuals, as well as for cities, countries, businesses, groups, and situations. They become the object of prayers and intercession. Intercession is coming between two things. We stand between the object of our intercession and God; or between the object and the devil.

When we intercede between the object and God, we make specific requests for provision, protection, direction, or blessings from God on behalf of the person, place, or thing for which we are praying. We also stand between the object and God in order to hinder and slow His judgment. In many cases, the only reason God has not sent judgment is because we are interceding on behalf of the world and those in it. Not that we are more merciful than God. He always longs to show mercy wherever possible. Our prayers give Him just cause to delay judgment and extend more opportunity for individuals to repent (Ex. 32:32; II Peter 2:9; Gen. 18:16-33).

## We Are a Threat to the Devil

As intercessors, our job is to stand between the devil and the people for whom we are interceding. This hinders what Satan would otherwise be able to do on the earth. We turn away his attacks, foil his schemes, and diminish his effectiveness.

This is why the devil expends so much energy trying to keep us preoccupied with ourselves. The powers of darkness would have us so focused on our own problems that we don't intercede for others. Satan would have us bound by fear, depression, lust, and materialism. He probably doesn't even mind us praying, as long as it is only self-centered. But at all costs, he wants to prevent us from interceding and obstructing his work in the world. We must see the threat we are to him as intercessors and recognize our significance in the earth as agents of God.

When we stand between the devil and the object of our intercession, we have to actively resist the powers of darkness. An example of intercession for an individual might be:

*Father, we come before you in the name of Jesus Christ and ask you to bring conviction upon this person and to lead him to repentance in his life. Satan, we come against you in the name of Jesus Christ and we cut off your influence in the life of this person in the areas of....*

The actual words we use are not as important as actually doing it. We need to understand what we are doing in the unseen realm and stand against Satan in the name of Jesus, forbidding him to act.

### Binding and Loosing

Jesus said, "Whatever you bind on earth will be bound in heaven, and whatever you loose on earth will be loosed in heaven" (Matt. 16:19 NKJV). We cut off the enemy from the object of our prayers (binding), and we pray down the Kingdom on the object (loosing). The Kingdom is simply where the King (Jesus) reigns. We "loose" by praying for the specifics of the Kingdom to fall upon the object—things like conviction, grace, love, and revelation. We bind the demonic forces from working and influencing, and we loose angels and God's Spirit to influence and work.

A question often asked me is, "Do we have to resist the devil every time we intercede?" No. Intercession can include spiritual warfare but doesn't always have to. We don't have to resist the devil every time we pray, but it is often included.

### Are You the Missing One?

God has chosen us as warriors in the name of Jesus Christ. If we have ever felt insignificant on this planet, we need only look at Isaiah 59. The first portion of Isaiah 59 describes society as we know it today. It describes unrighteousness, injustice, and evil in great proportions. Having described the evil in the world, Isaiah records God's reaction: "Now the Lord saw, and it was displeasing in His sight that there was no justice. And He saw that there was no man, and was astonished that there was no one to intercede" (Isa. 59:15-16).

Isaiah tells us that the Lord sees the evil in the world and He doesn't like what He sees. We need to be reminded that God sees everything. There is nothing which escapes Him. We get so worked up when we see injustice and evil in the world. We find it difficult to believe that God is as aware as we are. Yet He has never missed one sin, one harsh word, one lonely thought, or one injustice. He records it all in His infinite mind and feels the hurt of each one in His great Father's heart. God also has emotional reactions to what He sees. He is grieved and greatly displeased by that which cannot escape His notice. He doesn't like these things, nor condone them.

Too many think He is somehow unconcerned, and that what will happen, will happen. This, as mentioned earlier, is not a Christian concept. Islam says that whatever happens is Allah's will. How can we intercede for change in the world if we think terrible things are the will of God? The Bible is clear. God hates every evil and every selfish act of man.

God's feelings are our leverage in intercession. We intercede because we know God is not pleased with the way things are and is willing to bring change.

Verse 16 of Isaiah 59 then tells us that God saw there was no man and He was astonished that there was no one to intercede. Why was the eternal, omnipotent, sovereign God looking for a man? Is there anything He can't do? Couldn't He stop what was happening? Why would the Almighty God need a man?

### God Has Questions, Too

The whole world, Christians included, sees terrible things going on and says, "Why isn't God doing something about all this? Where is He?" The Bible tells us that God is asking questions of His own. He sees the evil and is astonished that there is no one interceding. "Where are the Christians? How can they be doing nothing?"

Why is God looking for a man? Why is He amazed when there are no intercessors? Because He knows the significance of intercession and the role of man on the earth.

God has established certain irrevocable principles in the universe. He will move in the affairs of mankind according to the degree and how specifically we pray. This is why God is looking for a man to intercede. This is why He is amazed when none can be found. God has all power. He has the love, and is fully willing to bring change in the world. But He stands astonished, even shocked, when we don't pray. God is crying out to His people: "I want to move. I want to bless. I want to save. I want to protect, provide, and stop injustice. Why won't you intercede?"

We must know without doubt that prayer changes things. It makes a difference unlike anything else we can do. Prayer changes things because God answers prayer. When we pray, God moves. God knows what He wants to do in the earth and in the lives of people around us. This is why God reveals His will to us and is specific when He does so. He wants us to pray according to His will. God even tells us what to pray. We wait on God; He speaks to us; we pray according to His will; and then He moves into action.

God is not limited, unable to do anything without man's prayers. God can do whatever He wants. He is sovereign. He is not bound by man. However, it seems that God has chosen to include man in the responsibility and authority of this planet. God has chosen to move in the affairs of man to the degree that we pray. God will not eliminate the middle man. There are certain areas in which God will not move unless we pray. And He is rightfully astonished when we don't.

Why don't we pray more? I believe it is because we are not convinced that our prayers really make a difference. And when we do pray, we far too often repeat words and sounds we've heard from others. We need to pray with firm conviction that our prayers will make a difference.

### A Prayer Guideline, Not a Ritual

When Jesus' disciples asked Him how to pray, He taught them what we call the Lord's Prayer. The Lord's Prayer is not so much a prayer as it is an explanation of how the earthly realm does business with the heavenly realm, and how heaven does business with earth. The Lord's Prayer is instruction for dynamic praying.

The Lord's Prayer in Matthew 6:9-13 begins "Our Father...." Jesus gave us permission to boldly approach God from an open, intimate Father-son basis. Jesus then said to pray, "Thy kingdom come" and "Thy will be done on earth." I am convinced that rather than just repeating His words, Jesus intended us to fervently press in. He wanted us to pray for God's will to be done and for His Kingdom to advance. He wanted us to pray for His will to be done in every area of our lives, in our family, in friends' and acquaintances' lives, in cities, countries, and in every situation.

### Thy Kingdom Come

Can we pray for God's Kingdom to be established in the earth? The Book of Revelation says that God will someday set up His Kingdom on earth. That is true and every word will come to pass, whether we pray or not. God will do what He has promised to do.

However, there is another aspect of the Kingdom of God— the Kingdom that is within every believer. (Luke 17:21) This is the Kingdom Jesus told us to pray into reality. It would have been a cruel joke if Jesus taught us to pray, "Thy kingdom come," knowing our prayers wouldn't make a difference. But our prayers do count. If we don't pray, the Kingdom won't come. And because we haven't prayed enough, the Kingdom of God is not in more than two billion people on earth.

### Thy Will Be Done

Is God's will being done on earth? This is a difficult question. If we say "yes," does this mean sin and evil are God's will? If we say "no," does it mean God is not in control of what is happening on Planet Earth? The answer is "yes *and* no." God does not will evil, sin, death, nor destruction in the earth. Neither is it God's will that Satan rule and influence as he does. God is, however, still in complete control. He is doing exactly what He said He would do. He is enacting His eternal purposes on the earth and is sovereign to move in any area. God chooses to act in the affairs of men through men, and in response to their prayers.

God hates sin. He stands against unrighteousness. People are perishing every day, yet God is "not willing that any should perish" (II Peter 3:9 KJV). He wants all men to be saved (I Tim. 2:4). We know they won't all be saved, but we can still see God's desires. He longs to establish His will in all who will respond to Him. However, there are many places and situations where God's will is not being done. This is why Jesus taught us to pray, "Thy kingdom come, Thy will be done, on earth as it is in heaven." He has given us the job of being watchmen...

> *On your walls, O Jerusalem, I have appointed watchmen; all day and all night they will never keep silent. You who remind the Lord, take no rest for yourselves; and give Him no rest until He establishes and makes Jerusalem a praise in the earth (Isa. 62:6-7).*

Isaiah 62, although referring to Jerusalem in another time, reveals a principle that can be applied to us today. I'm sure we've all heard someone say, "When you pray, only ask once. If you ask twice you will reveal a lack of faith." This is not in the Bible. In fact, the opposite is true. We are to ask and *keep on asking* until He answers or until He tells us we have asked enough. God may instruct us to stop after only the first time, and to trust in Him. The key is to pursue and obey God.

In Isaiah, God established "watchmen" or intercessors to pray all day and all night, petitioning God over and over again. We are to "remind the Lord"—to pray, giving Him "no rest until" our prayers are answered. God asks us to be unrelenting—not to let up until our prayers have brought results.

## Bible Prayers Were Bold

Many are afraid to bother God with requests. Our prayers become vague suggestions, like: "God, I'm sorry to bother You.

I know You're busy, but if You could, please...if it isn't too much trouble...if it is Your will....But if not, I understand...perhaps...maybe...." These are not the prayers we find in the Bible. The men and women of the Bible knew God and they knew who they were in God. They also knew that their prayers changed things in the world. They prayed bold, dynamic prayers which were forceful and direct. God has given us permission to pray with boldness and to pursue Him with vigor until He answers.

God is the One who has said, "Give me no rest." He's not going to be offended by our boldness. He might correct us if we pray with the wrong motive, but He is eager to hear and respond. Nehemiah, David, and others demanded of God that He listen. They reasoned with God. They wrestled with Him. This was not pride or arrogance. They simply knew God wanted them to pursue Him and to not let Him rest. Praying boldly and specifically is not a sign of disrespect. It comes from understanding the character of God, and what it is to be His child. God urges us, "Come on, give me no rest! I want to save and bless and heal and move. Come, and pray without ceasing!"

### A Challenge to Her Faith

Sometimes a Bible story makes us uncomfortable because we don't understand all that was going on in the situation. The story of the Canaanite woman in Matthew 15 is such a one...

> *And behold, a Canaanite woman came out from that region, and began to cry out, saying, "Have mercy on me, O Lord, Son of David; my daughter is cruelly demon-possessed." But He did not answer her a word (Matt. 15:22-23).*

Why did Jesus act that way? He lived a sinless life. He never acted out of selfishness. He was always compassionate and fair. Then why was He so seemingly rude to this Canaanite woman? Why didn't He respond? Here was a woman crying out in desperation, and God didn't answer.

How many times have we prayed and God has not answered? This may be difficult, but the Bible shows us that God sometimes delays answering our prayers. When God doesn't answer we get upset and out of sorts. We say, "It just doesn't work for me. God doesn't love me. It's no use. I might as well give up." And we walk away with less faith than we had before we prayed.

Jesus did not answer the woman. But notice this: She asked again. She didn't walk away discouraged; she pressed in and asked again. Jesus finally responded to her, but His answer inferred that she was a dog! This slur was characteristic of how the Israelites viewed the Phoenicians. Was Jesus being cruel? Was He a bigot? No. Jesus was just reminding her of her perceived position in their society. He knew the faith in her heart and was challenging it. It was a provocative statement that demanded a response.

She responded in verse 27, "Yes, Lord; but even the dogs feed on the crumbs which fall from their master's table." This woman didn't have the background of the Jews. She didn't know about all the heroes and stories of the Scriptures. But she knew what she wanted and she knew that Jesus could answer her prayer. Jesus praised the great faith of her reaction. Her faith was not in asking once, but continuing to ask, knowing that Jesus could and would heal her daughter. And He did just that.

Genuine faith will not give up, but will persevere. Prayers of faith are not praying once, but praying *until*. Sometimes God delays in order to provoke us to more prayer, because it is to the degree that we pray that God responds. God wants us to seek Him more diligently, regardless of circumstances, and regardless of delayed response.

### Shake Off Restraint; Be Shameless

In Luke 11:5-9, Jesus tells us a parable:

*And he said to them, "Suppose one of you shall have a friend, and shall go to him at midnight, and say to him, 'Friend, lend me three loaves; for a friend of mine has come to me from a journey, and I have nothing to set before him'; and from inside he shall answer and say, 'Do not bother me; the door has already been shut and my children and I are in bed; I cannot get up and give you anything.' I tell you, even though he will not get up and give him anything because he is his friend, yet because of his persistence he will get up and give him as much as he needs. And I say to you, ask, and it shall be given to you; seek, and you shall find; knock, and it shall be opened to you."*

Jesus chose the components of His parables precisely. Yet look at the incongruities of this story. Most of us would never go to our neighbor's house after they had gone to sleep to borrow food. It is not acceptable behavior. And to persist after the neighbor said, "Go away" would certainly be rude. This man shamelessly broke a number of social taboos. And yet it was his persistence that brought him what he needed.

Most of us could never bring ourselves to behave this way. However, God condones it, even encourages it when it comes to prayer. The last words of this verse have a literal meaning in the original Greek that is better translated: "Ask and keep on asking...seek and keep on seeking...knock and keep on knocking." Jesus was telling us in this parable to go beyond any restraint we have. We are to be shameless and not let any kind of conventions hinder our prayers.

## Keep On the Judge's Case

In Luke 18:1-8, Jesus tells us another story.

*Now He was telling them a parable to show that at all times they ought to pray and not to lose heart, saying, "There was in a certain city a judge who did not fear God, and did not respect man. And there was a widow in that city, and she kept coming to him, saying, 'Give me legal protection from my opponent.' And for a while he was unwilling; but afterward he said to himself, 'Even though I do not fear God nor respect man, yet because this widow bothers me, I will give her legal protection, lest by continually coming she wear me out.'" And the Lord said, "Hear what the unrighteous judge said; now shall not God bring about justice for His elect, who cry to Him day and night, and will He delay long over them? I tell you that He will bring about justice for them speedily. However, when the Son of Man comes, will He find faith on the earth?"*

Does Jesus find faith on the earth when His people will not endure in prayer? Jesus told us these stories that we might understand the significance of persistent praying. We must cling to God in our prayers and not let go until we see results. We are to pray and keep on praying, to shake heaven until we see responses to our prayers. Our diligence in prayer is not to wake God up, nor to beg Him, negotiate with Him, nor convince Him. He is already convinced and willing to help, to bless, and to save. This is His character. He is trying to wake us up, and convince us.

### Ask for Exactly What You Want

Not only should we be persistent in prayer; we should be forceful and specific. In Mark 10:46-52, we have the story of blind Bartimaeus. Jesus was heading out of Jericho when blind Bartimaeus heard He was coming. Bartimaeus yelled out at the top of his voice, "Jesus, Son of David, have mercy on me!" Everyone around him tried to hush him. He was disturbing the dignity of the occasion! But Bartimaeus "began crying out all the more." Not only did he not quiet down, he yelled louder and more often, "Son of David, have mercy on me!" Jesus finally walked over to this man and asked him, "What do you want Me to do for you?"

Jesus loves it when we are persistent and refuse to let Him go, even when we don't receive an immediate answer. He wants us to press in and keep praying. And He wants us to be specific. Jesus is still asking us today, "What do you want me to do for you?" We need to pray specifically, in detail—not vague, religious prayers that don't really tell God what we want. We must be specific in order for God to bring about specific answers. We don't always know all the details, but we should pray as specifically as we can.

Every Christian should pray with boldness, expecting God's response to every prayer. We need to give God no rest until our prayers have been answered. As we abandon our religious traditions and restraints, we can pursue God through prayer with unrelenting determination. If we become totally convinced that God moves in the affairs of men, then we will pray like this. And when we pray, we will see the hand of God move. We will see transformations all around us. Prayer will become one of the most exciting parts of our life. We will begin to shake our world. Society will feel the impact. People around us will change. We will become effective prayer warriors.

# CHAPTER TWELVE

## How to Wage Warfare

Spiritual warfare is not just a prayer prayed or a demon rebuked—it is a life lived. We've seen in the previous chapter how important prayer is. However, the Bible says in James 5:16, "The effective prayer of a righteous man can accomplish much." God linked praying with holy living—the way we walk. Everything we do either aids the forces of darkness or repels them. As we've said before, a defeated devil is effective only to the degree that people are sinning and living selfishly. It is exactly to that degree—no more and no less. Sin is what gives an opening to the devil. Ephesians 4:27 says, "Do not give the devil an opportunity."

In Jeremiah 5:1, God revealed both His merciful heart and the power of one righteous man. God told Jeremiah, "Roam to and fro through the streets of Jerusalem, and look now, and take note. And seek in her open squares, if you can find a man, if there is one who does justice, who seeks truth, then I will pardon her." God was prepared to stay His judgment of an entire city for only one righteous man.

Sodom and Gomorrah in Genesis 18:20-33 was a similar situation. Abraham pleaded with God not to destroy these cities, and asked God to spare them if fifty righteous people could be found. When God agreed, Abraham tried for forty righteous people. God again agreed and Abraham again tried for fewer. Finally, God agreed to spare the city if only ten righteous people could be found. God was not negotiating with Abraham, since

He already knew exactly how many righteous people there were. It was a discovery for Abraham to see just how wonderfully merciful God already was. God was always willing and always merciful. It also revealed to Abraham and to us the significance of even one righteous person.

### Effect on Society

Throughout history, there have been documented accounts of total revival. We tend to think of revivals as a series of meetings, but true revival is when an entire population is affected. For example, in Wales in the first decade of the twentieth century, over 100,000 were converted in a two-year period. The moral climate was so changed that taverns went bankrupt and police became unemployed. At least 80% of the converts were still in the Church five years later. [3]

Why doesn't this kind of spiritual awakening happen everywhere? Does revival take place because God happens to like a particular village more than others? The Bible says that God is no respecter of persons (Acts 10:34 KJV). He does not prefer one person above another, nor one village, city, or country above another. Then why are there whole villages that become saved and others don't?

This is the pattern of revival: God in His wisdom and sovereignty takes the initiative to convict; some respond to His moving. It may be only a few. When a large enough percentage of the people of God in that locality gets right with God and right with each other, He sees that conditions in a place make it wise for Him to pour out His blessing. Then it spreads outside the Church to the lost. The devil is driven back through the power of righteousness, and the Spirit of God descends, bringing conviction to everyone nearby. People's hearts and minds are opened to the Gospel. Some even get saved without anyone preaching to them.

This has happened countless times throughout history. This is revival brought on by the power of holy living.

---

3 Pratney, *Winkie, Revival*, Whitaker House, Springdale Pa., 1983

## Repentance as Warfare

Jesus told us that we are the "salt of the earth" and "the light of the world." He also warned us that salt can lose its savor, and light can be hidden under a bushel. We can be effective or ineffective. Our light can be a beacon to the world, or it can be hidden. As salt, our holy lives can change the flavor of the world, or we can go unnoticed and make no difference at all. For example, if we pray for someone struggling with a sin that is also present and unchecked in our own lives, our prayers will be powerless. But when we repent and pray, we smash the enemy's hold over people, pave the way for revival, and help establish the Kingdom of God.

It was during the World Cup Soccer Games in Argentina that I learned the power of repentance as part of spiritual warfare. John Dawson, Wick Nease, and I were the leaders of over two hundred workers in Cordoba—part of a nationwide outreach during the soccer games. But even though we had two hundred evangelists out on the streets of this city of ethnic Germans and Italians, we weren't making a dent spiritually. Every day we went out with literature, street preaching, and witnessing. But nothing happened.

John, Wick, and I met to pray. As we did, God began to show us that we were coming up against a stronghold of pride. The Holy Spirit likewise began to finger pride in each of our hearts. As the three of us humbled ourselves before one another, confessed particular areas of pride, and asked for God's cleansing, we became aware that this was why we were not being effective on the streets of Cordoba.

We three then went to our two hundred workers and humbled ourselves before them. After they responded, the Lord showed us His strategy for Cordoba: We were to go out in groups of 30 to all the main intersections and boulevards. Throughout that proud city, in front of elegant shops and cafes and in the financial district, we knelt down in obedience to God and asked Him for forgiveness. We humbled ourselves for our own sins and for those of the city.

There's nothing magic about kneeling on a street corner...unless God tells you to do it. We felt foolish, but we obeyed. And right away, we saw the change. The people of Cordoba became tender to our message, eager for the Gospel. In the next few weeks, people approached us, wanting to know how to be saved. They lined up for our literature; some even wanted us to autograph the tracts.

Repentance is a major weapon against Satan. It's simple: If I repent, I break the powers of darkness. But if I'm disobedient, I allow the enemy to work. If I obey God, I hold the devil off. If I'm moving in unbelief, I make room for him. But if I exercise faith, I cut him off.

## Physically Claiming Territory

Something happens when we go geographically and take an area for God. There is nothing particularly spiritual about traveling, being on a plane, or going on vacation. But when we go in obedience, filled with the Holy Spirit and walking in righteousness, we have an effect. Walking through an unrighteous part of town or stepping off a plane in a spiritually darkened nation can be an act of war.

In Joshua 6:1-20, Joshua and the children of Israel walked around Jericho for seven days, once every day for six days and seven times on the seventh day. Knowing human nature, by midweek a number were probably grumbling and wondering why God didn't just knock the walls down by Himself. Surely He didn't need them walking around in the hot sun to do the job. But they obeyed, day after day, putting one foot down and then the other. After seven days of physical obedience, the walls came down. Did the walls indeed fall because the children of Israel walked around them?

God could have knocked down those walls at any time, but He had greater things in mind. Israel was going to win more than one battle that seventh day. Through obedience and the very presence of the people of God, Israel drove back the powers of darkness in the unseen realm. God showed them the importance of going exactly where He wanted them to go, and doing exactly what He wanted them to do. Before the walls of Jericho fell, there was victory in the spiritual realm.

Man is not a passive bystander in the battle between light and darkness. God has delegated responsibility and authority to us. If we go and march, or go and preach, God will move. God knocked down the walls of Jericho, but only after His people did the marching.

Satan, as we learned earlier, deploys his forces geographically. We can have a greater effect on the principalities of a location by being in that place than by being elsewhere. This is why missions is so important and the reason why God calls His people to go, even for the short-term.

Over the years I have taken numbers of short-term mission volunteers to different nations. These teams are made up of ordinary Christians who want the opportunity to make a difference in the world. However, some have criticized the expense of these trips and have questioned their value. So I have gone before God many times to examine their validity.

What I believe the Lord has shown me is, when people join together with other believers far from their homes, something happens in the unseen realm. When they come serving and loving one another, preaching the Gospel, singing, worshiping, praising, and marching, the powers of darkness in that location take a beating like never before. It's not just traveling, but going in obedience to God that greatly affects the powers of darkness.

## Praying on Location

God is leading His Church to more and more praying on location as warfare. Many do prayer walks, going up and down the streets of their city, pausing as led by God at significant locations where major decisions are being made. Others have received understanding regarding spiritual "high places." Sometimes, as in Old Testament times, these are literally the highest places in a city; other times, they are not "high," but are places where there seems to be concentrations of evil.

We must be careful to get our strategy from God in each situation and place, rather than fall into tradition. Sometimes it is right to hit the strongholds first; at other times, smaller steps of obedience are needed first. In the Old Testament, God led His people to open confrontation with evil, like on Mount Carmel in I Kings 18. But in other instances, He said He world drive out their enemies a little at a time (Ex. 23:29-30).

Where past sins and practices have left a residue of evil, spiritual cleansing of an area or a building may be necessary. The idea of a haunted house is not fantasy. Many times locations need to have evil spirits driven out in Jesus' name.

A YWAM team in Chiang Mai, Thailand, once got a terrific bargain on a house, because the locals believed it was haunted. It did indeed have a spirit, but the YWAMers kicked it out in the name of Jesus and enjoyed living in that house for several years.

In many parts of the world, the land itself has been worshiped, has had curses put on it, and spirits invoked to it in the past. This has produced strongholds of evil. Also, many strongholds are due to a present day concentration of sin in a geographical area. God has led some Christians to redeem particular areas in prayer.

We must remember the importance of seeking God and being led by Him in any such activities. Not every piece of real estate needs to be cleansed. We shouldn't form a whole theology around rocks and trees and forget that it's people whom Jesus wants to save. We break bondages over territory only as these bondages relate to people, preventing negative influence over individuals in that area. As we become watchmen for our cities, nations, or institutions, we can daily cut off the evil influence in society:

> *Every morning I will destroy all the wicked of the land, so as to cut off from the city of the Lord all those who do iniquity (Ps. 101:8).*

### Preaching Is Warfare

Preaching cannot be separated from spiritual warfare. One sure way of getting rid of darkness is to turn on the light. Preaching the Gospel places light in the midst of darkness. If the Church has been called to anything, it is to preach the Gospel. We need to embrace every style and every method. If any presentation of the Gospel, no matter how innovative or old-fashioned, can be done in truth and in the love of Jesus, we need to do it. Some reject certain methods of evangelism—a young evangelist with a punk hairstyle and a rock band, or a man standing on a street corner with a megaphone. But if a method reaches one person who will only hear because of it, we need to do it. Of course we should also consider if anything we do is helping or hindering our preaching; but we should not discount any method. The devil will do all he can to talk us out of sharing the Gospel because he knows that preaching the Gospel drives back the powers of darkness.

## Reacting the Right Way is Warfare

Another way we wage spiritual warfare is through right reactions. Terrible things happen to good Christian people, as the Bible says, "Many are the afflictions of the righteous; but the Lord delivers him out of them all" (Ps. 34:19). Adversity is part of life in a fallen world and no one is exempt. The book of Job is a picture of calamities in the life of a faithful man. But Job's story shows us that we can have victory over the devil if we have the right reactions. Job lost everything and suffered every possible attack, both spiritually and physically. Yet Job defeated the devil. The attacks of the enemy didn't work. In the midst of all his suffering and confusion, although he didn't understand, Job was able to say with confidence, "I know that my Redeemer lives."

In any calamity, no matter how big or small, we have to acknowledge that we do not know everything. We don't know why things happen to us. But regardless of what happens, we should be able to say, "God is okay" (I Thess. 5:18; Prov. 3:5-6). Satan tries to prove to us that God fails us when our circumstances are less than ideal and even painful. We can react in hurt and bitterness toward God, or we can react with absolute trust in His character. Our circumstances do not change the wonderful character of God. We should never charge God foolishly or sin with our lips. We should never accuse God, criticize Him, blame Him, insult His character, nor complain about Him. If we charge God, we hand Satan a tremendous victory.

Every adversity is a prime opportunity for Christians to have a right reaction, to give glory to God, to uphold His character, and to defeat the devil. We are called to spiritual warfare, not a sheltered life of comfort without pain. Our comfort comes from knowing who God is. We are called to be overcomers, not avoiders. We are called to establish the Kingdom of God and resist the powers of darkness. God could remove us from the planet as soon as we're saved, but He chooses to leave us here to become spiritual warriors. We must live through suffering with right reactions. We must grit our teeth and endure adversity righteously to defeat the enemy's attacks.

## Setting Captives Free

Spiritual warfare certainly includes direct confrontation with demonized individuals at times. When Jesus said to go into all the world and preach the Gospel, He also told us to cast out demons in His name.

People develop bondage in their lives and need to be set free. We have the authority to do this and should do so wherever necessary. Not that we are to assume every human problem is some demon. We only need to ask God if there is a supernatural bondage at work.

Sometimes it is a combination of factors, supernatural and natural. A person could have deep-seated wounds which have given entry to demonic powers. In that case, in addition to casting out evil spirits, the wounds need to be healed in Jesus' name. Or, in other cases, the basic problem is the person's will. Does he really want to be set free? Is he willing to repent, forgive others, set himself against sin, and commit to the truth?

Deliverance should always be linked to repentance and healing. Demons are like flies—they swarm to wounds and corruption. We can either keep swatting the flies away, or repent of the corruption and heal the wounds. In order to remain free afterwards the newly-delivered person needs to be built up through the Word of God. This will give him strength to resist further advances and walk in victory.

Some think spiritual warfare is only deliverance. Others emphasize pulling down strongholds in the heavenlies. Still others say spiritual warfare is doing the works of Jesus—preaching, teaching, and living the truth. Yet another group claims all this is impractical. They claim we should focus on feeding the hungry, resisting racism, and speaking out against social injustice. I believe we have to do it all.

Pulling down strongholds is only important if people are led to Christ as a result. However, some are deaf to the preaching of the Gospel until we deal with hindering powers. And some can't break through into victory until bondage is broken in their lives. We must do it all as appropriate, and as God leads.

God had different strategies for each battle in the Old Testament. Jesus never used the same method twice to heal people. Stay out of a rut, and do anything the Holy Spirit leads you to do to meet the needs of people.

## Warfare Through Fasting

Fasting is a tremendous weapon against the enemy. Isaiah 58:6 says, "Is this not the fast which I chose, to loosen the bonds of wickedness, to undo the bands of the yoke, and to let the oppressed go free, and break every yoke?"

In the first chapter of this book, I told how God gave me steps to breaking spiritual strongholds in Papua New Guinea. That revelation came in a time of fasting and praying. When I went to start a YWAM ministry in Sydney, Australia, I was led to the eastern suburbs, which had little Christian witness. For thirty days, I fasted and prayed and walked those streets in spiritual warfare. Today, there are a number of thriving churches there. I couldn't have been the only one who prayed for a change in Eastern Sydney; but strongholds were certainly broken after a period of fasting and prayer.

Before joining Youth With A Mission in 1967, I was serving as an assistant pastor to Rev. James Nicholson in the state of Washington. We listened to a tape together of the exorcism of a young girl. It was quite dramatic, but one thing will always stay with me. When a Christian declared on the recording that they were going to fast and pray until she was delivered, the demon spoke out, "No, don't fast!" The Christian demanded, "Why not?" and the demon answered, "*It weakens us.*"

We cannot use the words of demons to formulate doctrine, but neither should we be afraid to report them. The Bible recorded the fact that demons cried out to Jesus that He was the Son of God. Fasting is an effective means of warfare.

## Giving as Spiritual Warfare

You may wonder what giving has to do with spiritual warfare. The Bible says in Malachi 3:10-11:

> "*Bring the whole tithe into the storehouse, so that there may be food in My house, and test Me now in this,*" *says the Lord of hosts,* "*if I will not open for you the windows of heaven, and pour out for you a blessing until there is no more need. Then I will rebuke the devourer for you, so that it may not destroy the fruits of the ground; nor will your vine in the field cast its grapes,*" *says the Lord of hosts.*

The devil is involved in the economy, right now. And this will increase. In the book of Revelation, we learn that when the incarnate devil comes, the Antichrist, he will be in absolute control of the economy. He will direct financial powers throughout the earth. The "mark of the beast" (Rev. 13:17) will be connected with buying and selling.

Satan is interested in finances. He knows the selfishness of man is inflamed by money. According to the Bible, the love of money is the root of all sorts of evil (I Tim. 6:10). This love of money affects every area of human existence. Greed is the very foundation of Satan's economic schemes. Therefore, the greatest weapon against this foundation is a giving heart. When people give, it totally frustrates Satan's attempts to influence people toward selfishness. Giving is contagious, undoing the work of the devil far beyond the act of a single giver. It ripples outward: With every gift comes a grateful heart, and with a more grateful heart comes a greater willingness to give. Giving initiates a cycle which can influence many.

God is not concerned about how much you have, but He is concerned about whether or not it grips your heart. He doesn't care how much you collect, but He does care how much you give. The issue for God is not wealth. The issue is your heart. You can be a billionaire and God will not be displeased. God doesn't want His people to be poor. He wants them to hold what they have in open palms, more willing to give than to receive.

Every week there are missionaries who have to leave the mission field because of lack of finances, while some churches and ministries spend millions irresponsibly. But we should never use the irresponsibility of some Christian workers as an excuse not to give to others. Giving in obedience to God is biblical, spiritual warfare that defeats the powers of darkness.

## Unity as Warfare

Unity is a powerful means of warfare and is one of the biggest factors in the unseen realm. Jesus said, "If two of you agree on earth about anything that they may ask, it shall be done for them" (Matt. 18:19). However, He was not referring to something that affects God's willingness to answer; He was showing us something that drives back the powers of darkness. The devil hates unity. This should be obvious by the amount of division, betrayal, undercutting, and factionalism he constantly sows among God's people.

When we fight and have any part in breaking up relationships—whether in a marriage, a church, or between different parts of the Body of Christ—we give the devil great advantage. The wolf will always separate the sheep to devour them. We must refuse to be any part of division. We must humble ourselves, put things right, forgive people, go the extra mile, and be tolerant. If we work for unity, it will keep the door shut to the enemy.

Jesus prayed for us to become one in His high priestly prayer in John 17. He knew the critical importance of unity in spiritual warfare, and asked the Father to protect us from the evil one in verse 15. I believe we open ourselves to many attacks of the evil one—sickness and even death—if we are in disunity.

However, as we stand together in solidarity, honoring one another, valuing one another, we are invincible. There is a multiplication and a broadening of power. "One shall put a

thousand and two ten thousand to flight" may be an indication
of the effect of unity in the heavenlies (Deut. 32:30).

## The Weapon of Signs and Wonders

When we deal with demonic forces, we are dealing with the
supernatural realm. Therefore, we should seek supernatural
manifestations of God's Holy Spirit through our lives—particularly the gifts of the Spirit revealed in I Corinthians 12. In John
7, Jesus spoke of the Holy Spirit as a force flowing like rivers
from our innermost being. Jesus didn't give any indication that
this kind of power should be rare, only given to a few scattered
spiritual heroes here and there. It was part of the equipping of
every Christian for warfare. This is why Ephesians 6:18 encourages us to pray in the Spirit, because there is an effect on the
forces of darkness. Every prayer has a spiritual warfare factor,
as the Holy Spirit flows through us, driving back the powers of
darkness.

I remember a time of witnessing on the beaches of Sydney,
Australia years ago, when we encountered a twelve-year-old
adversary. She was a young girl, but she was street tough, the
obvious leader of several other kids who hung about her. Each
day as we arrived at Maroubra Beach to witness, she would
follow us, shouting obscenities, interrupting our conversations
with, "Don't listen to these guys. They're full of ———!"

After several days of this, we prayed for her specifically.
The next time we came to the beach, there she was, leaning
against a rail smoking. She came over to us as we gathered
beside our van to pray, hurling her usual demonically inspired
ridicule. But this time, Iain MacRobert stopped her short: "Do
you know what your problem is? When you were three years
old, this happened to you...."

Iain gave several details of her life, when she was three
years old, six years old, and onward...specific things, including
family problems, and sexual abuse. Her mouth fell open and she
began to cry. "How do you know this stuff?" she demanded.
That day she and several others came to the Lord. The demonic
power was broken by the use of one of the gifts of the Holy
Spirit: the word of knowledge.

We should not hesitate to seek the Holy Spirit's wonderful and powerful manifestations. They can aid us in our warfare and drive back the powers of darkness.

## Serving Is Warfare

A surprising means of waging spiritual warfare is through loving service. The devil's nature is to steal, kill, and destroy (John 10:10). If we come in and meet the needs of those who have lost possessions, health, or home through war, disasters, or other tragedy, we are undoing the works of the enemy. Serving people in physical ways is not just a social gospel. It is a command from God and it is direct spiritual warfare. Loving service drives out the destroyers that attempt to bring despair and ultimately, death.

The enemy has strategies for destruction and he succeeds with thousands every day. The Church as God's representatives on earth can dramatically reduce the works of the enemy by meeting the basic needs of humanity. We must feed the hungry, house the homeless, visit the refugees, and assist disaster victims. This is effective warfare against the enemy, who always tries to take advantage of adversity.

## Acts of Faith Based on the *Rhema*

Yet another method of waging spiritual warfare is through steps of faith. Faith is not an emotional pressure that we muster in hopes that God will grant us our wishes. Faith is believing in who God is and in what He has said. Faith is based on the *rhema*, or specific, quickened Word of God to us at a particular time; and on the character of God as revealed in the *logos*, or written Word of God.

Hebrews 12:2 (KJV) says that Jesus is the author and the finisher of our faith. Whatever God begins, He will finish. When God says that something will happen, it will happen. However, we still need to do steps of faith—acts of obedience to what He tells us—to drive back the powers of darkness.

I live in Kona, Hawaii, near the campus of YWAM's University of the Nations. It is a beautiful property overlooking the blue Pacific. Its purchase was a story of spiritual warfare, requiring many steps of faith. Some didn't seem to make sense in the natural:

- God told the YWAMers to give personal, cherished items to one another to break the spirit of greed among those fighting to buy the property.

- The mission workers were led to camp out all night, taking turns sleeping on the ground with their families, while others kept praise vigils, thus reminding themselves that the Lord had always been the only One providing the roof over their heads.

- Loren Cunningham, the leader, had to make certain declarations to the judge during receivership proceedings—declarations which God told Loren to say, but which appeared quite foolish in the natural.

Three years passed. Finally, when the attorney came to finalize the agreements, he said, "Well, your God has given you the property!" It was God, but it was also specific acts of obedient faith on the part of YWAMers.

In I John 5:4 we learn of the power of faith: "This is the victory that has overcome the world—our faith." We need to be a people wholly dependent upon God, who seek His word, and wait for Him to bring revelation—the *rhema*. We need to hear God and step out in faith. As we do, we will defeat the powers of darkness who thrive on ignorance and unbelief.

We must guard against stepping back into a comfort zone where we only maintain our religious traditions. We can read the Bible, go to church, pray, and fellowship, but still be unwilling to hear God and step out in faith. In the comfort zone, we slowly cease to have conviction of who God is and what He has said. Without faith and our steps of faith, the world will overcome us, instead of our overcoming the world.

Everything we do should be based on the word (*rhema*) of God to us, because "faith cometh by hearing, and hearing by the word of God" (Rom. 10:17 KJV). If we do this, the rope of faith will be kept tight. If we pull hard in expectation, the enemy will be held at bay. Once we have received a word from the

Lord, we must continue to thank God for the answer, keeping active in our confession of faith. As it says in Colossians 4:2 (KJV): "Continue in prayer, and watch in the same with thanksgiving."

We all need to live by faith. Whether we have a million dollars or are totally broke, we need to live completely dependent upon God. A New York banker can live by faith as much as a missionary in the Amazon jungles. Living by faith is dependence upon God—waiting, listening, hearing, then acting. "Man shall not live on bread alone, but on every word that proceeds out of the mouth of God"(Matt. 4:4). Are we living by the word of the Lord? Are we living by faith? If we are, then we are holding back the powers of darkness.

## Warfare Through Praise

The Bible has much to say about praise defeating and driving back the powers of darkness. Second Chronicles 20 tells the story of Jehoshaphat, who was facing an enemy. Instead of sending out soldiers with swords and spears against them, he sent out "those who sang to the Lord and those who praised Him in holy attire, as they went out before the army and said, 'Give thanks to the Lord, for His lovingkindness is everlasting.' And when they began singing and praising, the Lord set ambushes against the sons of Ammon, Moab, and Mount Seir, who had come against Judah; so they were routed" (II Chron. 20:21-22). As Jehoshaphat's praise warriors raised their voices to God, angels were sent to defeat a physical foe. The physical enemy was defeated because unseen enemies were scattered by the power of praise.

Praise isn't merely a nice way to begin a meeting. It's not a warm-up or filler, nor Christian tradition. Praise is not just an activity, like singing or raising our hands. Praise is from the heart and should never be done lackadaisically. If praise is just something we do mechanically, it truly is meaningless. But biblical praise drives back the powers of darkness, releases the angels of God to do battle on our behalf, and brings God's awesome presence into each situation.

Psalms 149:5-6 declares, "Let the godly ones exult in glory; let them sing for joy on their beds. Let the high praises of God be in their mouth, and a two-edged sword in their hand." This Scripture accurately describes the movement of the Holy Spirit in and through the Church in recent years. A resurgence of praise and worship and teaching of the Bible—the two-edged sword—has characterized every growing, vibrant church throughout the world today.

The problem is that we have seen these as ends in themselves. We think of worship and teaching as the substance of a healthy, mature Christian life. We go to church for worship and teaching, and we go to schools, camps, and retreats for worship and teaching. But the often overlooked truth of Scripture is that worship and teaching are not the end. They are means to an end. We do these things in order to accomplish something greater. Otherwise, we are in danger of losing our focus and becoming self-serving.

The reason we are committed to worship and teaching is not to get blessed and filled up, but "To execute vengeance on the nations, and punishment on the peoples; to bind their kings with chains, and their nobles with fetters of iron; to execute on them the judgment written" (Ps. 149:7-9). Through worship and the proclamation of the Word of God, we bring God's judgment on the kings of darkness, binding them with chains.

Worship and teaching the Word are spiritual warfare, defeating the enemy and releasing the forces of light into the world to establish God's kingdom. The reason we exist is not just to have big, happy churches. We are to live and worship and proclaim the Word of God to the nations and peoples of the earth. This will drive back the powers of darkness and implement every intention of the heart of God.

## Verbally Opposing the Devil

As mentioned earlier, another way to wage spiritual warfare is by directly rebuking the enemy. "Submit therefore to God. Resist the devil and he will flee from you" (James 4:7). We should aggressively deal with the enemy—as Jesus did in the wilderness—verbally opposing the devil and using the Word of

God to counter his attacks. Jesus told us to bind the strong man, and then we could spoil his goods (Matt. 12:29). The "strong man" is simply the predominating demonic influence in any situation; and we are to eliminate that influence. It can mean the difference between life and death.

Some years ago, Darlene Cunningham, wife of YWAM's founder Loren Cunningham, had an experience which drove home the importance of this. While living in YWAM's first center in Switzerland, Darlene was standing on wet concrete in the laundry room, unloading her clothes from the washer to the dryer—both industrial size. In Europe, the current for such machines is 350 volts.

When an article fell behind the dryer, Darlene reached for it, not knowing that workers had removed its protective panel to repair it earlier. When her hand touched an exposed wire, her whole body convulsed. She found herself pinned, helpless as 350 volts shot through her. "God help me! Jesus help me!" she cried out, but still the surges coursed through her body.

Knowing she was seconds away from death, Darlene prayed again. "Why isn't it working, God?" she cried. "Why aren't You answering me?" Instantly the Lord responded, "Bind the devil, Darlene." The moment she spoke out against Satan, Darlene was hurled off the live wire and slammed against the opposite wall.

It took several days for the rhythm of Darlene's heart to return to normal, but she was okay. Even the inch-wide hole burnt into her palm by the live wire eventually healed without scarring. But Darlene never forgot the lesson of that day in the laundry room.

**The Last Weapon**

We are a generation of quitters. We quit our places of leadership. We quit our marriages. We drop out of church. We get hurt and discouraged and quit. Don't we realize that this is part of the warfare? "For you have need of endurance, so that when you have done the will of God, you may receive what was promised" (Heb. 10:36). Satan is in constant hope that God's people will give up—that their circumstances, the tasks set before them, and the daily adversities of life will be too much for them to endure.

The winner will always be the one who doesn't give up. If we stick it out, the devil won't. If he knows that we will endure, he will give up all the sooner. Sometimes the only effective weapon, and often the last to be employed, is just saying, "I'll die before I let this thing go!" Or, to use the words of Scripture, "They overcame him...they did not love their life even to death" (Rev. 12:11).

It is this weapon of endurance that finally convinces the devil that he has to give up. Too many Christians quit minutes before the victory.

By looking at the many ways to do spiritual warfare, we can see that it encompasses the entire Bible message and the whole of Christian life. Wouldn't it be wonderful if Christianity were simply God and us in a perfect universe? We could just sit before Him, working on our imperfections and being daily transformed into the likeness of Christ. Wouldn't it be wonderful to never have to consider sin, the devil, evil in the world, or personal adversity? We are not far from realizing this kind of life. It is a promise from God for the future of every Christian. It will be a reality when we get to heaven. But to pretend that this is what Christianity is today, in this life, on this planet, is a destructive escapism. We live in a fallen world, and we face an incredibly evil, deceptive enemy. We encounter trials, tribulations, temptations, and every form of adversity. The world around us is lost, starving, languishing under tyranny. We cannot escape or deny these things.

However, these are temporary. Life on this earth is but a snapshot in eternity—a minute portion of time. And yet this flash of time is the focal point for God and all His creation. Though short, the battle being waged in the realm of man is pivotal for the future. Victory is not in question, but who shares in that victory is.

We are the primary combatants upon whom rests the future. This is not to exclude God. He is our Creator, our Lord, and our victorious Savior. He is our strength and our hope. He has ensured the conquest of the powers of darkness. Nevertheless, He has chosen not to leave us out. He has delegated responsibility to us. He has chosen us as co-workers in the establishment of His Kingdom and the destruction of the kingdom of darkness. God is waiting for His people to rise up and take hold of the victory He purchased on the Cross. He desires that we reach back to the Cross by praying in Jesus' name and bringing that total victory into every space and time situation.

Spiritual warfare is a life lived. It is embracing the truth and living daily, aware of the enemy and committed to God. It is knowing that God has left it up to us. If we do not drive back the powers of darkness, they will not be driven back. If we do not rebuke the enemy, he will not be rebuked. If we do not reduce the evil in the world, it will continue to grow.

Spiritual warfare is not a fragment of Christianity. It is the whole of the Christian experience. It encompasses everything we do. To be a Christian is to be a spiritual warrior. To be a spiritual warrior is to walk consistently and victoriously through life, with Christ at our side.

# OTHER LIFE-CHANGING BOOKS AND CASSETTES FROM DEAN SHERMAN AND YWAM

**Dean's Tape Albums:**

- "Relationships," an album of 6 audio cassettes ($24.95 US)Dean challenges us to live and walk in right relationships.

- "Spiritual Warfare," an album of 12 audio cassettes ($39.95 US)Dean explores the many dynamics and strategies of spiritual warfare.

**Other YWAM Books:**

- *Is That Really You, God?*, by Loren Cunningham with Janice Rogers ($6.95)
  The story of a young man with a big dream. That dream was Youth With A Mission. Repeatedly, as Loren Cunningham worked to see his dream fulfilled through thousands of young people carrying the message of Jesus Christ to every continent on the globe, he encountered opposition and difficulties. Often he was driven to his knees to question, "Is this dream really from You, God?" Seeing it become reality put Loren through some tough lessons—lessons that can help you learn to know the voice of God and run with the dream He has given you.

- *Anchor in the Storm*, by Helen Applegate with Renee Taft ($6.95 US)The gripping true story of how Helen and her husband Ben, former captain of the mercy ship, M/V Anastasis, persevered through insurmountable odds to hold on to their dream to serve God on the high seas.

- *Daring to Live on the Edge: The Adventure of Faith and Finances*, by Loren Cunningham with Janice Rogers ($6.95 US)A compelling, fresh look at the subject of faith and finances by one of America's premier missions statesmen. This book will challenge and equip all who want to obey God's call, but who wonder where the money will come from.

- *The Father Heart of God*, by Floyd McClung ($5.95 US)Floyd, Executive Director of YWAM, shares how to know God as a loving, caring Father and a healer of our hurts.

- *Father Make Us One*, by Floyd McClung ($6.95 US)Knowing that biblical unity is not always easy, this book shares keys for loving others, even when it is hard.

- *Intimate Friendship with God*, by Joy Dawson ($6.95 US)Keys to knowing, obeying, and loving God by this dynamic teacher.

- *Leadership for the 21st Century*, by Ron Boehme ($7.95)At the close of the century, how will you lead? A great book with the goal of changing the nations through the power of serving.

- *Living on the Devil's Doorstep*, by Floyd McClung ($7.95)Join Floyd and his wife, Sally, in urban missions with YWAM, as they live first in a hippie hotel in Kabul, Afghanistan, and then next door to prostitutes, pimps, drug dealers, and homosexuals in Amsterdam, Holland.

- *Personal Prayer Diary-Daily Planner* ($11.95 US)What you get: quiet time journal, daily agenda, weekly goals, systematic Scripture readings, unreached people groups to pray for, prayer journal, concise teaching section, 9 pages of maps, and much more.

- *Spiritual Warfare for Every Christian*, by Dean Sherman ($7.95 US)Spiritual warfare is for everyone! It's more than rebuking demons—spiritual warfare is a life lived. Dean's classic teaching is now a book.

- *Taking Our Cities for God*, by John Dawson ($7.95 US)New bestseller on how to break spiritual strongholds. John Dawson gives you the strategies and tactics for taking your cities.

- *Target Earth*, by University of the Nations/Global Mapping Int'l ($27.95 US)This 170 page, full color atlas is filled with facts, maps, and articles by some fifty contributors.

- *Walls of My Heart*, by Dr. Bruce Thompson ($8.95 US)Dr. Bruce's popular teaching, now in book form, deals with the wounds and hurts that we all receive, and how to receive biblical healing.
- *We Cannot but Tell*, by Ross Tooley ($6.95 US)How to evangelize with love and compassion. Great for group studies as well as personal growth. Learn to reach out from your heart.
- *Winning, God's Way*, by Loren Cunningham with Janice Rogers ($6.95 US)Winning comes through laying down your life. This book gives the reader a look at the Cunningham's personal struggles and victories. A classic teaching of YWAM.

For a complete catalog of books and cassettes, write to the address below. To order any of the above listed books, write the title and quantity desired and send with the amount in US dollars.

FREE shipping at book rate with your order from this book.

Youth With A Mission Books
P.O. Box 55787
Seattle, WA 98155 USA
tel. 206/771-1153

## About the Author and His Ministry

Dean Sherman is Dean of the College of Christian Ministries at Youth With A Mission's University of the Nations in Kona, Hawaii. He is respected internationally as a Bible teacher, having taught since the 1970s in minister's conferences, YWAM schools, and churches in 49 states and in more than 40 countries. Twenty-five thousand sets of his teaching series in audio and video tapes have sold in 17 languages.

Dean helped to pioneer YWAM ministries in New Zealand, Fiji, Tonga, Australia, and New Guinea. He has served on the leadership council for YWAM in Asia and the Pacific, and continues in an advisory capacity for this region of missions endeavor. He and his wife Michelle and their two children live in Kona, Hawaii, where they lead missionary training schools. They often travel with ministry teams into Asia and the Pacific.

**Youth With A Mission and the University of the Nations**

Youth With A Mission is an international, interdenominational Christian mission reaching out to the world with the Gospel of Jesus Christ through evangelism, training, and mercy ministries. YWAM has 7,000 full-time staff and annually trains approximately 25,000 short-term workers to minister in over 390 operating locations in 100 countries.

The University of the Nations has as its primary aim the equipping of men and women to be communicators of the Gospel to all peoples of all nations in response to Christ's Great Commission found in Matthew 28:18-20. It has 150 training locations worldwide, and an international staff and student body. The original campus is located in Kona, Hawaii, where Dean Sherman lives and teaches.

**For more information** on short-term missions opportunities, or training with YWAM's University of the Nations, write to:

Youth With A Mission, 75-5851 Kuakini Highway, Kailua-Kona, Hawaii 96740 —tel. 808/326-7228